Drugs, insecurity and failed states:
The problems of prohibition

Nigel Inkster and Virginia Comolli

D0815800

Drugs, insecurity and failed states: The problems of prohibition

Nigel Inkster and Virginia Comolli

IISS The International Institute for Strategic Studies

The International Institute for Strategic Studies

Arundel House | 13–15 Arundel Street | Temple Place | London | WC2R 3DX | UK

First published March 2012 by **Routledge**
4 Park Square, Milton Park, Abingdon, Oxon, OX14 4RN

for **The International Institute for Strategic Studies**
Arundel House, 13–15 Arundel Street, Temple Place, London, WC2R 3DX, UK
www.iiss.org

Simultaneously published in the USA and Canada by **Routledge**
270 Madison Ave., New York, NY 10016

Routledge is an imprint of Taylor & Francis, an Informa Business

© 2012 The International Institute for Strategic Studies

DIRECTOR-GENERAL AND CHIEF EXECUTIVE Dr John Chipman
EDITOR Dr Nicholas Redman
ASSISTANT EDITOR Janis Lee
EDITORIAL Dr Jeffrey Mazo, Carolyn West, Dr Ayse Abdullah
COVER/PRODUCTION John Buck
COVER IMAGES iStockphoto

The International Institute for Strategic Studies is an independent centre for research, information and debate on the problems of conflict, however caused, that have, or potentially have, an important military content. The Council and Staff of the Institute are international and its membership is drawn from almost 100 countries. The Institute is independent and it alone decides what activities to conduct. It owes no allegiance to any government, any group of governments or any political or other organisation. The IISS stresses rigorous research with a forward-looking policy orientation and places particular emphasis on bringing new perspectives to the strategic debate.

The Institute's publications are designed to meet the needs of a wider audience than its own membership and are available on subscription, by mail order and in good bookshops. Further details at www.iiss.org.

Printed and bound in Great Britain by Bell & Bain Ltd, Thornliebank, Glasgow

British Library Cataloguing in Publication Data
A catalogue record for this book is available from the British Library

Library of Congress Cataloging in Publication Data

ADELPHI series
ISSN 1944-5571

ADELPHI 428
ISBN 978-0-415-62706-1

Contents

ACKNOWLEDGEMENTS

This book benefited immensely from the exchange of ideas that took place over the course of two workshops in October 2010 and April 2011. The authors are particularly grateful to the experts who actively took part in these exercises and those who made time to share their views and expertise during private meetings.

Successful field research has been made possible by a number of individuals and organisations in the United Kingdom, Colombia and Ghana, among which the following deserve special mention: The Embassies of Colombia and Mexico in London, General Oscar Naranjo, head of the Colombian National Police and his staff, the Bogota office of UNODC, Drs Daniel Mejia and Salomon Kalmanowitz of the University of the Andes, The National Planning Agency and Presidency of Colombia, the Serious and Organised Crime Agency (SOCA), the British High Commission in Accra, Dr Kwesi Aning, the West Africa Network for Peacebuilding (WANEP), the Prevention of Aids And Drug Abuse Foundation (PADF), the staff of Remar Ghana, the staff of the African Centre for Peace Building (AFCOPB), the Narcotics Unit of the Ghanaian National Police, Dr Axel Klein, and a number of people who prefer to remain anonymous.

The authors owe a special thank you to Danny Kushlick from Transform Drug Policy Foundation for his help and feedback throughout the project, and to Torbjorn Soltvedt, Xavier Servitja, Michael George and Alex Castro, who provided research assistance during different phases of the project.

The project would not have been possible without the generous financial contribution of the Open Society Foundations and the Global Drug Policy Programme in particular.

GLOSSARY

ANA	Afghan National Army
ASNF	Afghan Special Narcotic Force
ATPA	Andean Trade Preference Act
ATPEA	Andean Trade Preference Extension Act
ATS	Amphetamine-Type Stimulants
AUC	Autodefensas Unidas de Colombia
BACRIM	Bandas Criminales Emergentes
CARSI	Central America Regional Security Initiative
COIN	Counter-Insurgency
CPS	Concentrate of Poppy Straw
CSTC-A	US Combined Security Transition Command–Afghanistan
DEA	US Drug Enforcement Administration
DFID	Department for International Development
DFS	Direccion Federal de Seguridad
DRC	Democratic Republic of the Congo
ECOSOC	UN Economic and Social Commission
FARC-EP	Fuerzas Armadas Revolucionarias de Colombia – Ejercito del Pueblo
FATF	Financial Action Task Force
ICOS	International Council on Security and Development
IDU	Intravenous Drug Use
IED	Improvised Explosive Device
INCB	International Narcotics Control Board
ISAF	International Security Assistance Force
MCLN	Movimiento Civico Latino Nacional
MFN	Most Favoured Nation

MS-13	Mara Salvatrucha
NGO	Non-Governmental Organisation
NTM-A	NATO Training Mission – Afghanistan
ONDCP	US Office of National Drug Control Policy
PNC	National Civilian Police (El Salvador)
PNR	Partido Nacional Revolucionario
PRM	Partido de la Revolución Mexicana
PRI	Partido Revolucionario Institucional
PRT	Provincial Reconstruction Team
NSP	Needle and Syringe Exchange Programme
SACEUR	Supreme Allied Commander Europe
UNAMA	United Nations Assistance Mission to Afghanistan
UNDCP	United Nations Drugs Control Programme
UNDP	United Nations Development Programme
UNGASS	United Nations General Assembly Special Session
UNODC	United Nations Office on Drugs and Crime
WHO	World Health Organisation

INTRODUCTION

There can be few subjects that are debated with such passion as the international trade in illegal narcotics. The debate, driven as it is by a complex array of moral, ethical and ideological factors, many of which cannot be quantified, raises some fundamental questions about individual liberties and the rights of governments to constrain these liberties. Few governments have countenanced challenges to the prohibition-based approach to narcotics governed by the three international conventions.[1] Indeed, the commitment of major Western powers to this regime extends to the provision of financial aid and military training for beleaguered governments in producer and transit states, often to the detriment of human security in those countries. But even if attitudes were to change, establishing a clear factual basis on which to assess what is currently an illicit trade is by no means straightforward.

There are many psychoactive substances that have been declared illicit and therefore subject to an international prohibition regime that is probably more uniformly observed than any other international treaty in existence. Beyond these illicit substances are a growing number of so-called 'legal highs' and the increasing problem of abuse of psychoactive medicines available on medical prescription to deal with pain, depression and stress. There are also substances such as alcohol and tobacco, which enjoy widespread social acceptance and are marketed subject to varying degrees of government regulation, since their consumption can have adverse health and social consequences. Among all these substances, two particular classes of narcotic stand out for their sheer power and addictive properties: opiates – including opium itself and various chemical derivatives such as morphine and heroin – and coca-based products, predominantly in the form of cocaine. The impact of these drugs on health and social order has preoccupied policymakers since the mid-twentieth century. More importantly, however, these substances have played an important part in enabling and perpetuating some intractable conflicts in areas of the world that are vulnerable to destabilisation, with consequences that go beyond the areas in which these conflicts occur.

Heroin, or diacetylmorphine, was first synthesised by British medical researcher C.R. Alder Wright in 1874 in St Mary's Hospital, London. It was not developed commercially until 1895, when diacetylmorphine was independently synthesised then marketed by the Bayer Corporation, under the trade-name heroin. Initially it was believed that heroin would resolve the problem of addiction to morphine, a naturally occurring alkaloid of the opium poppy (*Papaver somniferum*) which had been widely used as an analgesic and anaesthetic since the mid-nineteenth century. In the event, it became clear that heroin was far more addictive than morphine, being up to ten times as powerful. Like all opiates, heroin has a chemical structure that closely mimics naturally occurring opioids such as endorphins, enkephalins and dynorphins, receptors for which are found in the brain, spinal cord and bowel. It is delivered quickly from the blood to the brain, where it turns into morphine and binds to the mu-opioid receptors. In effect, the morphine acts as a depressant to the central nervous system, by flooding the space between the nerve cells and preventing neurons from firing. Heroin is typically injected, either intravenously or subcutaneously – known as 'mainlining' – but it can also be smoked, a process known as 'chasing the dragon'.

Cocaine is a naturally occurring alkaloid found in the coca leaf (*Erythroxylum coca*). First isolated in 1860 by Albert Niemann and Paolo Mantegazza, cocaine was synthesised in 1898 by Richard Willstaetter and marketed shortly thereafter by a number of Western pharmaceutical companies. It can be injected – as any reader of Arthur Conan Doyle will be aware – but is more commonly snorted in the form of powder or smoked in a form known as 'crack'. In contrast to heroin, cocaine stimulates the central nervous system by first releasing, then inhibiting the re-uptake of neuro-transmitters such as serotonin and dopamine, giving rise to prolonged feelings of euphoria and well-being. The release of neurotransmitters such as dopamine is a natural function of the body's mesolimbic reward pathway – a system which essentially promotes certain behaviours such as eating and sex by associating them with feelings of pleasure. Such a lesson-learning mechanism, while having obvious evolutionary benefits, has perverse consequences when the wrong lessons are learnt, as happens when a user of powerful psychoactive drugs develops an overwhelming compulsion to keep recreating the sense of peace or euphoria associated with their use.

The problem of dependence is particularly acute in the case of heroin. Once neurons that have long been suppressed by the action of heroin begin firing again, changes in the brain chemistry take place which lead to severe physical withdrawal symptoms. These include cramps, nausea, severe anxiety, fever, diarrhoea and muscle spasms, which can last for up to 14 days. Though severe, such symptoms are rarely fatal. Cocaine withdrawal, though producing none of the physical symptoms of heroin withdrawal, can give rise to symptoms such as depression, fatigue and anxiety. In such circumstances a resumption of cocaine use can induce feelings of paranoia rather than the expected high.

Drugs in general, and heroin in particular, have been identified with all kinds of harmful effects. The 2010 UN Office for Drugs and Crime's World Drugs Report, for example, stated that:

> More users of heroin die each year from problems related to heroin use, and more are forced to seek treatment for addiction, than for any other illicit drug. Among illicit narcotics, opiates are also the most costly in terms of treatment, medical care and arguably drug-related violence. In addition, heroin is the drug most associated with injection, which brings about a host of acute and chronic health problems, including the transmission of blood-borne diseases such as HIV/ AIDS and Hepatitis C.[2]

None of what the UNODC says is incorrect. But what it fails to make unquestionably clear is that the adverse affects cited are largely a consequence of the fact that heroin is illicit. Hence users are forced into an underground existence dominated by the need to obtain their next fix by whatever means, even resorting to crime and high-risk behaviours such as prostitution. For those who are trapped in this cycle, issues such as drug purity, hygiene and general health may be very much secondary considerations. Heroin in and of itself causes none of the problems listed by UNODC. Rather, taken at controlled levels of purity and in a sterile environment, it is a relatively safe drug that can be consumed long-term without significant ill effects – not that this constitutes an argument in favour of recreational use. In 2010, a group of British doctors led by former Home Office drugs adviser Professor David Nutt published a paper in the *Lancet* medical journal arguing that alcohol caused far more harm in the United Kingdom than either heroin or crack cocaine, taking into account the public health, social and economic factors associated with alcohol abuse.[3] Prof. Nutt had been dismissed from his advisory position in 2009 for challenging the basis on which the British government sought to reclassify certain drugs including cannabis and ecstasy – placing them in a higher category in terms of potential harm and enabling harsher penalties for possessing or dealing the drugs – a stark illustration of the degree to which the public debate is affected by considerations other than the strictly scientific.

The same tendency towards polemic is evident in the debate about other illicit drugs. This is particularly true in respect of cannabis, recently 'upgraded' under the UK classification system from Class C to Class B. The UNODC estimates anywhere between 129 and 191 million people smoke cannabis.[4] Most appear to do so without significant adverse consequences and many physicians regard cannabis as less harmful than alcohol. But there is some evidence that cannabis, particularly the more potent variants such as 'skunk', may increase the risk of psychosis in adolescents whose brains are still developing – although the evidence for this is far from conclusive and needs to be assessed in the light of a decline in the general incidence of psychotic ailments such as schizophrenia.[5] It has also been alleged in the media that cannabis functions as a 'gateway' drug, leading users to experiment with and become addicted to more potent drugs. Such a claim, though intuitively plausible, is hard to substantiate.

Ecstasy (methylenedioxymethamphetamine, or MDMA), has gained notoriety in the UK following a relatively small number of fatalities, given its popularity among teenage nightclub-goers. These deaths were apparently due to extreme overheating and organ failure resulting from the effects of drinking too much water (hyponatraemia) following excessive physical activity, rather than to any particular pharmacological property of the drug itself. Prof. Nutt controversially described taking Ecstasy as being no more dangerous than riding a horse, an activity that results in around ten deaths and 100 traffic accidents each year in the UK. He and his colleagues on the Advisory Council on the Misuse of Drugs recommended that ecstasy be downgraded to Class B, to reflect their view on the level of harm it posed to individuals and society. Yet the British government has continued to classify Ecstasy as a Class A drug, putting it on a par with substances such as heroin and cocaine.

What is clear is that taking any but the mildest of psycho-active substances entails a degree of risk and that the consequences of taking such risks are unpredictable. As the US Drug Enforcement Agency website puts it, 'you can't predict the effect that a drug will have on you ... Everybody's brain and body chemistry are different. Everybody's tolerance for drugs is different.'[6] While in broad terms the way in which psychoactive drugs work is increasingly well understood, it is still not known why some people are able to experiment with or consume in moderation psychoactive substances without becoming addicted, while others succumb to addiction. The impulse of society and governments to protect their populations, in particular the younger element more disposed to engage in risky behaviour, is entirely understandable. Whether a prohibition-based approach is the most effective way of doing so is something which will be explored in subsequent chapters.

The size of the drugs trade

There are two principal sources of information and statistics on the size of the international narcotics trade: the UNODC and the United States Office of National Drug Control Policy (ONDCP). The UNODC, which is regarded as employing a more rigorous methodology, relies on statistics compiled by national governments but is also directly engaged in efforts by the main producer states to monitor the extent of illegal cultivation and production of drugs. These efforts are inevitably limited in scope due to the fact that most areas of production are under the control of armed groups hostile to the state. The ONDCP conducts its own satellite surveys of drug-producing areas but does not supplement these with on-the-ground investigations.

The discrepancies that arise between the two approaches are epitomised in an article by Colombian economists Daniel Mejia and Daniel M. Rico on the micro-economics of cocaine production and trafficking in Colombia.[7] The authors point out that, according to UNODC statistics, the area of coca cultivation in Colombia more than halved between 2000 and 2008 from 163,000 to 80,000 hectares, whereas ONDCP estimates give totals for the same years as respectively 140,000 and 119,000 ha. Estimates for the amount of cocaine production in 2008 are respectively 430 metric tonnes (UNODC) and 295 metric tonnes (ONDCP), though Mejia and Rico estimate that the figure for potential production could lie anywhere between 440 and 840 metric tonnes with a probable average of 642 metric tonnes.[8] The proposition that a smaller area of cultivation can produce more cocaine than a larger area is one that will be dealt with at greater length in a subsequent chapter, but can in essence be explained by cultivation techniques designed to produce greater yields per coca bush.

The uncertainties in respect of production are reflected at all stages in the supply chain. As the head of Colombia's

National Police, General Oscar Naranjo, has observed, interdiction statistics are subject to double counting, with producer
and consumer states both claiming the same seizures.[9] And
when it comes to retail sales in consumer countries, the picture
is further blurred by the propensity of dealers to cut their
product with a range of more or less noxious substances, to
the point where levels of purity and hence availability and
value become hard to ascertain. The UNODC has suggested
that seizure levels would need to be consistently at 75% of total
production in order to inflict sustained damage on the traffickers' business model. Optimistically, annual seizures are
reported as amounting to 40% of total production. But since we
have only the haziest idea of the quantities of illegal narcotics
produced or consumed in the world, or what the value of this
trade amounts to, it is impossible to know how much is truly
taken out of circulation.

For working purposes, most analysts rely on the figures
produced by the UNODC in reports produced annually since
1999, which at least offer some basis of comparison and hence
insight into global trends. The UNODC is itself cautious about
the limitations of its approach, pointing out for example that
its annual reports on what it calls the 'world drug problem'
describe a problem for which there is no internationally agreed
definition. It also concedes that, according to its own methodology, some 12,000 metric tonnes of opium (which would
equate to 1,200 metric tonnes of heroin) apparently produced
in the period 2008–09 simply cannot be accounted for. But the
broad trends it depicts are instructive. Over the past 30 years
the world has witnessed a significant and sustained increase in
the amount of opium produced in the world, from 1,000 metric
tonnes in 1980 to a peak of 8,890 metric tonnes in 2007, declin-
ing to 4,000 in 2010. The majority of this (at least 85%) emanates
from Afghanistan, with a significant increase beginning after

the Soviet withdrawal in 1989. The total value of this market is assessed at US$65 billion, 85% of which is accounted for by heroin. The picture for cocaine is more stable, with annual estimated production at 774 metric tonnes in 1990 and 865 metric tonnes in 2008. The estimated value of the global cocaine market is US$88bn, which represents a 50% drop since 1990.[10]

Establishing levels of usage is an even bigger challenge, since by definition consumers of illegal drugs who do not inadvertently come to the attention of their national authorities through either the public health or criminal justice systems are unlikely to wish to advertise their consumption choices.

Demand for drugs is very lumpily distributed around the planet for reasons that are not understood. It is not obvious why 22% of New Zealanders should have admitted to using cannabis whereas only 0.05% of Japanese have made a similar admission. Or why British people appear to consume so much more cocaine than French people. Determining elasticity of demand is also difficult, since demand is governed by so many factors including availability of alternative substances and such nebulous concepts as fashionability. The UNODC claims that the collective efforts of the global community have limited the consumption of illegal narcotics to around 200 million people (some 0.5% of the global population), though it offers no evidence for its contention that without such efforts, levels of consumption would be much higher. Of this number around 11m are estimated to be heroin users and somewhere between 15m and 19m are cocaine users. Since most heroin users are by definition problem users, as are many of those consuming highly addictive crack cocaine, this figure represents an obvious concern to the governments of those countries – mainly in the developed Western world – that have to deal with it. But it arguably pales into insignificance when compared with those aspects of the international narcotics trade that most directly impact on global security, namely the security implications for producer and transit states and the emergence of non-state groups linked to the narcotics trade which are able to challenge the authority of nation states and otherwise exercise international strategic effect.[11]

The power of such groups has been eloquently described by former UNODC Executive Director Antonio Maria Costa as one of five unintended consequences of the international drugs control regime.

> The first unintended consequence is a huge criminal black market that thrives in order to get prohibited substances from producers to consumers. Whether driven by 'supply push' or 'demand pull', the financial incentive to enter the market is enormous. There is no shortage of criminals competing to claw out a share of a market in which hundred-fold increases in price from production to retail are not uncommon.[12]

This thought was further developed by the UNODC as it launched its 2009 World Drugs Campaign: 'Criminal organisations have the power to destabilise society and governments ... Collusion between insurgents and criminal groups threaten[s] the stability of West Asia , the Andes and parts of Africa, fuelling the trade in smuggled weapons, the plunder of natural resources and piracy.'[13] The nature of the market for illicit drugs is such that most of the profit is made at the top of the production chain; in the case of cocaine, over 80% of the profits are believed to remain in consumer countries. The table below illustrates the cost structure of cocaine and heroin.

What these figures dramatically illustrate is that the major profits in this business accrue to those who control the international trafficking routes and retail distribution networks,

Table 1. **Prices of cocaine and heroin through the distribution system c. 2000 (US$ per kilo)**[14]

Stage	Cocaine	Heroin
Farm gate	$650 (coca leaf in Colombia)	$550 (opium from individual farmers in Afghanistan)
Export smugglers/traffickers bringing large quantities across international borders	$1,000 (Colombia)	$2,000–4,000 (Afghanistan)
Import smugglers/traffickers bringing large quantities across international borders	$15,000–20,000 (Miami)	$35,000
Wholesale (kilo) wholesalers handling large quantities of drugs in consumer countries	$33,000 (Chicago)	$50,000 (London)
Wholesale (oz) lower-level wholesalers selling smaller quantities to retailers	$52,000 (Chicago)	$65,000
Retail (per 100mg pure; retailers selling directly to users)	$120,000 (Chicago)	$135,000 (London)

Sources: European Communities, 2009, based on data from DEA, EMCDDA, UNODC and Matrix Knowledge Group, 2007. © European Communities, 2009.

those areas where the risk is greatest and where there is most need for organisation. There are many recreational drugs apart from heroin and cocaine, and creative chemists are constantly coming up with new variants of legal highs designed to circumvent existing prohibitions. But perhaps yet more worthy of attention are heroin and cocaine, because of the unique role these lucrative commodities have played in both fomenting and sustaining high levels of insecurity in vulnerable states.

CHAPTER ONE

The evolution of the international drugs trade

The long history of the drugs trade began with the production and use of cannabis, opiates and coca leaves for both medical and religious purposes. Opium and cannabis were cultivated in the Mediterranean region from the Neolithic era (7000 BCE to 3000 BCE) and the chewing of coca leaf in the Andean region of Latin America can be dated back to c. 1000 BCE.

For most of recorded history the use of such stimulants tended to be the preserve of social elites, but the breakdown of traditional hierarchies during the Age of Exploration gave rise to more widespread consumption. This was especially true of the Andean region of Latin America, where Spanish colonists were quick to perceive the benefits of paying a pressed Indian labour force in coca leaf. The United Kingdom was responsible for developing the systematic cultivation of opium from plantations in British India which, in the early nineteenth century, it began exporting to China, leading to the so-called Opium Wars. The nineteenth century witnessed a significant increase in drug use in the developed Western world generally – but particularly the US and UK – where opiates and coca-based products were freely available and widely marketed. During this period, advances in chemistry led to the production of opiate and coca derivates such as morphine, heroin and cocaine, which were medically more efficacious but also far more addictive than the substances they replaced. To begin with they were equally widely marketed. A Sears Roebuck catalogue from the 1890s offered a cocaine kit complete with hypodermic syringe for $1.50. Until the early twentieth century, cocaine was an active – though relatively minor – ingredient of Coca-Cola.[1]

As the use of narcotics grew, so too did concern on the part of national governments about their effects on society, prompting the introduction of various regulatory measures (see Chapter Four for more details) aimed at curbing production, trade and consumption of drugs. One of the unintended consequences of banning measures was the emergence of illicit markets to fulfil the ever-increasing demand. An early example of this dynamic was witnessed in China in the late eighteenth century, when Imperial edicts banning opium imports led to a network of smugglers competing with each other to control significant portions of the market.[2] In the West, early instances of restrictions imposed on drugs were motivated in part by growing public health concerns but also by a desire to protect national pharmaceutical industries. In the late nineteenth and early twentieth centuries, colonial powers such as Germany and the Netherlands invested considerable resources in the production of cocaine for medical purposes from coca bushes grown on Javanese plantations, which produced higher alkaloid yields than their Andean equivalent once chemists had learnt to make use of both crystallised and uncrystalised alkaloids to produce cocaine.[3] This trend even gave rise to protectionist impulses, with tariff barriers being applied to coca exported from Latin America. It was not until the twentieth century that Western countries came to be preoccupied by the social and economic consequences of unrestricted use of narcotics, prompting a move away from a laissez-faire approach to self-medication towards imposing controls over addictive substances, often based on moral preconceptions which labelled addicts as deviants.[4]

It was, however, another psychoactive substance, alcohol, which was the subject of the West's first formal ban. The Volstead Act, in force from 1919 to 1933, was the culmination of more than a century of pressure from religious groups in the US which viewed the consumption of alcohol as a sin. This view increasingly coincided with contemporary expectations about the need for citizens in modern industrialised states to take greater responsibility for their health and standards of personal conduct. The main consequence of the Volstead Act was the creation of an enormous criminal black market dominated by gangs from Italian, Irish and Jewish immigrant communities still marginalised and to a degree stigmatised by mainstream US society. Bootlegging – as the smuggling of illicit alcohol came to be known – gave rise to significant levels of criminal violence as different groups fought turf wars, and to widespread corruption within US law enforcement, the judiciary and the political classes. Nor did these new criminal gangs restrict themselves to bootlegging; they also expanded into areas such as gambling, loan-sharking, bookmaking, extortion, prostitution and drugs, in particular heroin from France, the Middle East and Southeast Asia, which was used to keep prostitutes compliant and dependent. By the time the Volstead Act was repealed, America had witnessed the creation by New York mafioso Salvatore 'Lucky' Luciano of the modern world's first truly transnational criminal cartel, characterised by high levels of organisation and a collaborative rather than competitive approach between different criminal groups.

Though Luciano was eventually imprisoned in 1936 on charges of running organised prostitution, his luck did not desert him. A 1943 agreement to use his mafia contacts to smooth the way for Allied forces about to embark on their invasion of Italy led, three years later, to his release from prison and deportation to Italy. From there he built a major criminal enterprise which involved morphine base smuggled from Turkey via Lebanon to laboratories in Sicily and the French port of Marseilles, from whence the resultant heroin was shipped to the US.[5] 'The French Connection', as it became known, continued more or less uninterrupted until the mid-1970s, at which point the very structured and hierarchic nature of the Mafia contributed to its downfall at the hands of US law enforcement. As a consequence of the Vietnam War, heroin was from the late 1960s trafficked into the US from the Golden Triangle area covering Burma, northern Thailand and Laos, where it had been cultivated since the mid-nineteenth century. During the first and second Indo-China wars, both French and US forces secured the services of the Hmong hill tribes as scouts and guerrillas against the Vietcong by facilitating the shipment of the tribes' opium harvest from the Laotian segment of the Golden Triangle. In the case of France, this was achieved with the assistance of Corsican criminal groups; in the case of the US, it was Air America, acting on behalf of the CIA, that flew the opium to Bangkok where Sino-Thai criminal gangs refined it into heroin. (This was not the last time US strategic interests were to predominate over what was to become a 'War on Drugs'. For a brief period in the 1970s, the US intelligence community looked the other way while Nicaragua's Contras smuggled cocaine to Miami until Congressional funding for the rebels was approved.[6]) By the late 1970s, a combination of prolonged drought and political instability led to a marked reduction in heroin imports from the Golden Triangle in favour of heroin trafficked from the Golden Crescent – Turkey, Afghanistan and Pakistan – which remains the main source of much of the world's heroin supply.

As demand for both heroin and cocaine grew in the US between the 1960s and 1980s and thereafter in the more affluent states of Western Europe, the number of organisations dedicated to meeting this demand grew in number and variety, as did the routes by which the narcotics were transported. Cuban criminal groups smuggling narcotics into Miami for the US market were eventually displaced by Colombian groups, firstly in the form of the highly organised and vertically integrated Medellin and Cali cartels, and then by a range of so-called 'boutique' cartels, equally highly organised but characterised by a more flexible, horizontal structure and a readiness to outsource aspects of the business to other groups, such as the Mexican cartels who took over control of the transit routes. Heroin has been smuggled into the US by both Colombian and Mexican groups as well as the European criminal gangs referred to earlier. The European cartels of the French Connection era have since been supplanted by a multiplicity of actors, each of which tends to dominate one stage of the transaction chain. Thus heroin will be smuggled out of Afghanistan by Afghan criminal groups, transported across Central Asia by local groups and then handed to Turkish criminal groups who bring it into Europe for distribution by local criminal gangs. Increasingly, cocaine is smuggled from Latin America to Western Europe via West Africa, from whence local criminal groups ship it northwards.

Globalisation and the rise of transnational organised crime

By the early twentieth century, the process of globalisation had evolved as far as the then-available technology would permit. The development of drugs – promoted up until this point by nation-states rather than criminal groups – was an adjunct to this process of globalisation, which appeared to have reached a plateau in the period immediately prior to the First World War. Following a long hiatus, globalisation was given a major fillip as the collapse of the Soviet Union opened up new markets, at the same time as advances in communications technology and the availability of affordable air travel brought these markets within easy reach. Just as was true for licit commercial activity, so the international narcotics trade, now exclusively in the hands of organised criminal groups, derived major benefits from the new dispensation. Nor was the activity of such groups confined to narcotics, though these still constituted the lion's share of criminal entrepreneurship worldwide. Criminal gangs increasingly moved into trafficking licit but heavily taxed commodities such as cigarettes, people (globalisation may have liberalised trade and financial flows, but the flow of labour is still subject to substantial restrictions), pornography and counterfeited goods of various kinds. As Misha Glenny has observed of the changing world order that emerged from the Cold War:

> One group of people, however, saw real opportunity in this dazzling mixture of upheaval, hope and uncertainty. These men (and occasionally women) understood instinctively that rising living standards in the West, increased trade and migration flows and the greatly reduced ability of many governments to police their countries combined to form a goldmine. They were criminals, organized and disorganized, but they were also good capitalists and entrepreneurs, intent on obeying the laws of supply and demand. As such, the valued economies of scale, just as multinational corporations did, and so they sought out overseas partners and markets to develop industries that were every bit as cosmopolitan as Shell, Nike or McDonalds.[7]

This new generation of organised criminal groups was able to flout national boundaries and exploit differences in political and legal systems in different states to its own benefit. As the opportunities grew, so too did the number of individuals and groups becoming involved with a focus on those forms of illicit enterprise offering the highest returns for the lowest risk. This diversification led to a further erosion of the archetypal, vertically integrated hierarchic model of criminal organisation exemplified by the Mafia and Colombia's Medellin Cartel, in favour of more flexible, decentralised structures; it represented a shift from the 'directed network' to the 'transaction network',[8] whose members were defined by their loyalty to the enterprise in hand rather than to personal relationships or ethnic origin. This more flexible model acquired some of the characteristics of a classic espionage network, in which increasingly specialised cell-based areas of activity operated in ways designed to distance them from the higher echelons of the network who were thus less vulnerable to law-enforcement action.

A further characteristic of transnational organised crime is the degree to which the licit and illicit economies intersect. Over time, many major criminals have sought to 'go legit', both in order to diversify their portfolios and to achieve a degree of social acceptance which involvement in purely criminal enterprises cannot readily confer. Moreover, some forms of organised crime are so lucrative – and this is particularly true of the cocaine trade – that criminals in the upper echelons of the trade literally have a problem knowing what to do with their money. Such was the case with Medellin Cartel boss Pablo Escobar – a classic example of a gang boss who aspired to social mobility – who burned bundles of dollar bills to keep warm at night while on the run from Colombian authorities.[9] Organised criminal groups have funnelled increasing amounts of money into the licit economy through a process of money laundering estimated by the UNODC to account for 2–5% of global GDP.[10] The fact that money once laundered is indistinguishable from that earned through legitimate entrepreneurial activity significantly blurs the distinction between the licit and illicit economies and raises intriguing questions about how governments should deal with such revenues. Beginning with the creation in 1990 of the Financial Action Task Force (FATF), international initiatives to counter money-laundering have proliferated to the point where the sheer multiplicity of institutional arrangements has begun to be seen as a potential handicap.[11] These initiatives have undoubtedly served a useful purpose in helping governments to better understand global financial flows and to deal with issues such as the funding of transnational terrorist groups. Their effectiveness against organised criminality per se is, however, harder to determine.

Perceiving a direct challenge to the sovereignty and authority of nations states, politicians and security officials became increasingly alarmed. Initially, the debate came to be dominated by the mistaken belief that a few large, vertically integrated criminal organisations were in control of global markets in illicit goods and services. Typical of the formulations to be found in this period was the following observation: 'Transnational criminal organisations pose serious threats to both national and international security, and are extremely resistant to efforts to contain, disrupt, or destroy them.'[12] Senator John Kerry published a book positing the convergence of organised crime and terrorism as the major new security threat faced by the US.[13] In 1996 US President Bill Clinton, in Presidential Decision Directive 42, characterised international organised crime as a threat to the security interest of the United States and directed appropriate US government agencies to enhance and co-ordinate their work against this threat. The United Nations Convention Against Transnational Organised

Crime was signed in Palermo in 2000. In a foreword to the convention, then UN Secretary-General Kofi Annan summed up the threats posed by transnational organised crime as

> terrorists, criminals, drug dealers, traffickers in people and others who undo the good work of civil society. They take advantage of open borders, free markets and technological advances ... They thrive in countries with weak institutions ... they are powerful, representing entrenched interests and the clout of a global enterprise worth billions of dollars.[14]

This perception of transnational organised crime as a national and international security threat evolved at a time when the whole concept of national security was undergoing extensive re-evaluation in the aftermath of the Cold War, reflecting Barry Buzan's comment that 'security is anything but a constant'.[15] As Buzan pointed out, concepts of national security have varied through time and, in the post-Cold War environment, security came to be seen as encompassing the economic, political, societal and even environmental dimensions as well as the more traditional military-focused concept of national security. The 1994 Human Development Report by the United Nations Development Programme (UNDP) introduced an additional concept of human security, which equated security with peoples rather than national territories and which took economic development as its primary focus.[16] Within this context, a preoccupation with the phenomenon of transnational organised crime could be seen as entirely legitimate. But initially it gave rise to a one-size-fits-all securitised approach which has arguably had some highly undesirable implications for those states and peoples most vulnerable to the impact of this phenomenon and least well equipped to respond to it. In so doing, some aspects of the threat as conceived by developed Western states have actually become more salient as the transnational implications of events in remote parts of the world translate into externally generated security threats.

As has already been observed, transnational organised crime is a phenomenon which sits at the intersection of the licit and illicit worlds and derives much of its benefit from being in that unique location. And the impact of such activity on governance and social stability can vary significantly depending on the characteristics of the society which is affected and the nature of the criminal activity involved and how this is perceived. Peter Lupka has evolved a well-known scale for describing the nature of interaction between criminal groups and the state which ranges from predatory, where the criminal groups are in an antagonistic relationship with the state; to parasitic, where criminal gangs achieve limited engagement with the state and are able to suborn parts of it; and finally to symbiotic, where a relationship of mutual dependence exists between criminal groups and the state.[17] Generally speaking it is in the interests of criminal groups to move beyond the predatory stage as quickly as possible, as this stage imposes significant costs and constraints on the business model – though in the case of Colombia's Pablo Escobar, dealt with in more detail in Chapter Two, a parasitic relationship was allowed to deteriorate into one that became predatory, with fatal consequences. As Mats Berdal and Monica Serrano have observed, prohibition is normally the catalyst which enables a parasitic relationship between criminal groups and the state.[18]

Although there are examples in the developed world of symbiotic relationships between governments and organised crime networks – Italy's Social Democrat Party and the Mafia, Japan's Liberal Democrat Party and the yakuza – generally speaking, levels of parasitism and symbiosis are less evident in states with good standards of governance and strong institutions. That is not to say that organised crime does not jeopardise the security of states in the developed world. The prevalence of illicit goods and services provided by criminal groups has the potential to erode social standards. The methods used by such groups to enable and protect their business interests, in particular the corruption of law enforcement, judiciaries, civil servants and politicians, has the potential to degrade the effectiveness of institutions and erode all-important public trust. Poor and more vulnerable elements of societies in these countries are disproportionately vulnerable to the more malign and disruptive social impact at a local level of organised criminal activities such as drug selling and prostitution. This is especially true for recent immigrant communities, who often subsist on the margins of the state and have little recourse to state institutions. But as a general rule, the harms inflicted by organised criminal groups are more evident and have greater impact in states suffering from poor governance, weak institutions and conflict, and where the licit economy is unable to meet the needs of populations.

Organised crime and conflict

The interrelationship between organised criminality and conflict has become an increasing feature of the modern era. It reflects the changing nature of armed conflict: warfare between nation states has become a rarity; civil war is in relative decline; while various forms of conflict and violence abound which, in the words of the 2011 UN World Development Report, 'do not fit neatly into either "war" or "peace" or into "criminal violence" or "political violence"'.[19] Such forms of violence are to be found in many parts of Central America and the Andean region, sub-Saharan Africa, Central and South Asia, the Caucasus and, during the 1990s, the Balkans. As the World

Development Report goes on to observe, endemic violence and instability affect 1.5bn people around the world and have a significant detrimental effect on economic and human development.

The role of criminality in perpetuating conflicts, by providing the material resources for its continuation and thereby entrenching interest groups whose wealth and power becomes dependent upon continuing state instability, has been analysed in depth by scholars such as Paul Collier and Anke Hoeffle.[20] Of particular relevance has been the realisation that conflicts fuelled by trafficking in commodities typically last much longer than others. According to James L. Fearon, 'conflicts where rebels relied extensively on contraband financing had a mean duration of 48.2 years as compared to 8.8 years for other conflicts'.[21] Numerous commodities have featured in this dynamic: cigarettes in the Balkans; diamonds in West Africa; rare earth elements and minerals in the Democratic Republic of the Congo (DRC); tropical hardwood in Cambodia; cocaine in Colombia and Central America; and heroin in Afghanistan. The role of diasporas in perpetuating conflict through the generation of criminal revenues has also been a growing characteristic of conflicts in the late twentieth and early twenty-first centuries: Kurdish and Sri Lankan Tamil émigré groups have been involved in various forms of extortion and fraud in the UK, Canada and France in order to raise funds for their fighters.[22] In many cases, the antagonists lose sight of the original *casus belli* as revenue generation becomes their primary purpose. In some cases, trafficking requires a degree of complicity by other states and non-state groups, such as transnational corporations not involved in the conflict. This is particularly true of commodities such as rare earths and minerals, the transportation routes and destinations of which are limited and in principle subject to surveillance and interdiction. Concerted international action has proven effective in one case, the Kimberley Process, set up to tackle the problem of blood diamonds. But criminal behaviour has on more than one occasion been condoned by elements of the international community. Both European states and the US were willing to turn a blind eye to Montenegro's status as a major centre of cigarette smuggling between 1996 and 1998, in the interests of eroding support for the Serbian regime of Slobodan Milosevic.

Situations of conflict tend to be seen in black and white terms; good versus bad, legal versus illegal. But the reality is that such situations present ambiguities beyond those which typically apply in peacetime. As James Cockayne and Daniel Pfister have observed:

> Often these situations cannot be reduced to a simple, binary opposition between legitimate state organisations and illegitimate criminal organisations. Such analysis is particularly problematic where a state exists in name only, is fragile or engages in behaviour which calls its own legitimacy into question at the international or local level. In many cases it may even be hard to distinguish on the ground between what is legal and what is criminal. Many state-backed criminal law norms will lack popular legitimacy in areas affected by conflict ... And in many conflict situations, government entities and criminal organisations come to resemble each other, providing similar services – especially protection – financed by similar rents and taxation arrangements.[23]

Cockayne and Pfister go on to argue that post-conflict reconciliation may well require the integration into the new dispensation of the many of the illicit actors whose activities may have fuelled the original conflict, as is evident in the case of Afghanistan.

What's special about narcotics?

But although narcotics are not the only commodity that can create the conditions for and sustain conflict, there are reasons to treat them as a commodity which is, in some important aspects, *sui generis*. Within a climate of global prohibition, illicit coca and opium-poppy cultivation can only occur in locations where governance is weak or non-existent, or where, as is arguably the case in Afghanistan, criminal entrepreneurs have achieved a level of 'state capture' amounting to symbiosis. Narcotics can be grown in numerous locations; coca leaf can be grown in some 30 countries; licit opium poppy for medical purposes is grown in locations as diverse as Australia and southern counties of England. In circumstances where the state is effectively unable to function or provide social or economic services for its citizens, coca and poppy cultivation become a form of social insurance and a store of value. With narcotics cultivation may also come a degree of physical security, since it is in the interests of narcotics traffickers to ensure minimal disruptions to the cultivation process and to farmers. Narcotics respond to the three characteristics identified by Michael L. Ross as critical in determining their role in conflict perpetuation: lootability, obstructability and legality.[24] The low obstructability of drugs is particularly relevant; there is virtually no limit to the methods whereby they can be trafficked, and a focus by law enforcement on specific routes or concealment options simply results in relocation and diversification. Demand for the products is constant if not rising, and the considerable profits to be made, which are to a large extent a function of the risk created by a prohibition regime, constitute a significant incentive for traffickers.

Since the 1980s, illicit narcotics have had a significant adverse impact on levels of national and human security in the developing world. That effect continues to feed through into new areas. As Chapter Two will illustrate, a particularly toxic combination of narcotics-related crime and insurgency brought the Colombian state to the brink of failure, and left that country with a formidable legacy of economic and social problems, not the least of which is the continued production of drugs. Afghanistan has seen a process of state capture in which significant elements of the current Afghan administration are deeply engaged in the narcotics trade and see the expansion of the state as a direct threat to their financial interests and power bases. The interests of the latter paradoxically coincide with those insurgent groups who rely, inter alia, on revenues from the opium trade to sustain the insurgency. Pressure by the governments and law-enforcement agencies of consumer countries may have had some limited impact on the governments of producer states, but the main function of such pressure has been to spread the problem of narcotics trafficking more widely. As Chapter Three will demonstrate, pressure on Colombian narcotics cultivation and trafficking has led to a major upsurge of narcotics-enabled criminality and insecurity in Mexico – where the breakdown of a long-term symbiotic relationship between traffickers and the state has resulted in surging levels of violence – and in some of the states of Central America, whose stability is now threatened by narcotics-fuelled gang violence. And as trafficking routes have diversified, some West African states have shown themselves particularly vulnerable to 'state capture', with all the threats that this poses to the development of robust and effective institutions.

The perception that high levels of violence in the developed world are a consequence of an excessive focus by the international community on supply rather than demand has led to a degree of pushback by some of the states most affected by narcotics-fuelled violence. In February 2009, former presidents Fernando Henrique Cardoso of Brazil, Cesar Gaviria of Colombia and Ernesto Zedillo of Mexico issued a statement to the effect that the so-called War on Drugs, with its focus on supply, had been a failure. This statement, seemingly a response to alarming levels of narcotics-related violence in Mexico made the point that

> the revision of US-inspired drug policies is urgent in light of the rising tide of violence and corruption associated with narcotics. The alarming power of the drug cartels is leading to a criminalisation of politics and a politicisation of crime. And the corruption of the judicial and political system is undermining the foundations of democracy in several Latin American states.[25]

The three former presidents have since produced a report of the Global Commission on Drug Policy, launched on 2 June 2011 in New York, calling for a revision of the assumptions underpinning global counter-narcotics policies and re-focusing effort towards demand management. In essence, the three presidents were reflecting a growing perception in producer states that it was no longer reasonable to expect such countries to shoulder the security burden of a policy prompted by self-indulgent and hedonistic behaviour in the developed world. Chapters Four and Five will examine the impact of a prohibition-based regime and the potential for alternative approaches, including those advocated by the commission.

CHAPTER TWO

Prohibition

By the turn of the twentieth century the world seemed awash with opiates and coca-based drugs. Opium had become a major factor in the economics of Western imperial policy, in particular that of the United Kingdom, France and the Netherlands. The Opium Monopoly in British India accounted for 20% of government revenues. In Malaya revenue from opium sales met 53% of the UK's colonial administration costs and in the Dutch colonies of Java and Sumatra the figure was 15%. In 1907, global opium production was estimated at 41,624 metric tonnes.[1] Coca leaf was being cultivated commercially in a range of colonial territories including British Guyana, India, the Dutch East Indies, Jamaica, Malaya and Ceylon to supply a burgeoning pharmacological industry based primarily in Germany and Switzerland. Countries such as Turkey and Persia continued to cultivate significant quantities of opium poppy to meet traditional medical and recreational requirements. China had 700,000 acres of land under poppy cultivation and close to 3% of its population addicted to opium. Meanwhile, in Western countries, opiate addiction that was caused by medical treatment (iatrogenic) and a consequence of self-medication was becoming a matter of increasing public concern. As William B. McAllister has put it,

> by the early twentieth century, Western societies generally viewed unrestricted drug availability and use with concern. The older notion that psychoactive substances, the individual and social setting contributed equally to drug-related problems had given way to an emphasis on the drug as the key agent engendering negative consequences … By the early twentieth century, the question was not whether access to drugs ought to be regulated, but what level and type of regulation was appropriate.[2]

In fact, early vestiges of a move towards regulation had been evident well before the turn of the twentieth century. These were driven by a complex array of motives. Concern for public health was a factor, as realisation grew that many of the patent medicines so prevalent in the late Victorian era contained substances that were actively detrimental to human health. But other factors came into play: morality, at the time focused more on alcohol, which was seen as a greater threat; and also racism. This was particularly true in respect of the US's Chinese community, which had settled on the West Coast after taking part in the construction of the Pacific Transcontinental Railroad. Efforts driven by US labour unions to discourage this community from settling, or at least expanding led in 1875 to San Francisco's ordinance banning the smoking of opium, then seen as a quintessentially Chinese vice (laudanum, or tincture of opium, widely used for self-medication, was not included in the ban). Racism was to remain a significant factor in the history of drug control within the US, with urban myths abounding about the extent of crimes committed by 'drug-crazed Mexicans and Negroes'.[3]

It was, however, the US's reluctant assumption of imperial responsibilities following the 1898 Spanish–American War which gave rise to the first specific step in a process leading to the current international regime. As a consequence of the war, the US had inherited responsibility for Spain's colonial possessions, including the Philippines where, in common with the rest of Southeast Asia, opium smoking had become endemic. Under pressure from Charles Brent, the Episcopal Bishop of Manila, the US Congress enacted legislation empowering the Philippines government to prohibit the importation or sale of opium for other than medical purposes.[4] And in 1909, pressure from Brent led President Theodore Roosevelt to convene the Shanghai Opium Commission with the maximalist aim of outlawing the use of opium for anything other than medical or scientific purposes. Morality apart, Roosevelt was keen to gain political credit with the Chinese government and to enhance the prospects for US companies to do business in China by eliminating a commodity which absorbed so much Chinese spending power. Faced with objections from the major European powers, the commission failed to reach any agreement. But two years later, agreement in principle was reached at the Hague Opium Convention on medical need as the sole criterion for opiate production, even though at that point it proved impossible to reconcile the highly divergent interests of US moralists, Western imperial powers and states engaged in the manufacture of opiate and coca-based pharmacological products in a way that would effectively operationalise this aspiration. The Hague Opium Convention saw the beginnings of a US approach that focused exclusively on supply reduction because, as McAllister has observed, 'the principal enforcement efforts fell on other governments'.[5] The US Senate ratified the Hague Convention with uncharacteristic alacrity. And in 1914 the US introduced the Harrison Act, ostensibly a taxation measure but in reality designed to restrict the consumption of opiates by limiting access to them. Over time, the act was used to prosecute physicians providing maintenance doses of drugs to addicts, effectively cementing the beginnings of a domestic prohibition policy.

In the aftermath of the First World War, international efforts to gain further purchase on the drugs trade became focused on the League of Nations, which the United States refused to participate in despite its being established largely through the efforts of US President Woodrow Wilson. The first major achievement of the league was the International Opium Convention, which took place in Geneva in 1925. The convention imposed obligations on states to make regular reports to the newly established Opium Advisory Committee and Permanent Central Opium Board on levels of consumption, imports, exports, manufacture, production and stocks of opiates, coca-based products and, for the first time, cannabis. And it had the power – at least in principle – to impose an embargo on drug imports or exports on any state failing to meet its reporting obligations, including non-signatories. The convention also established a system of schedules for classifying drugs according to their potential harms. The International Opium Convention was reinforced by the 1931 Convention for Limiting the Manufacture and Regulating the Distribution of Narcotic Drugs. This set a global ceiling on demand for manufactured drugs based on states' estimates of medical need and required signatory states to set up national drug-enforcement agencies to ensure compliance with national counter-narcotics legislation. The effect of the 1931 convention was to draw a clear line between the trade in licit narcotics and illicit trafficking. The latter phenomenon was explicitly addressed in the 1936 Convention for the Suppression of the Illicit Traffic in Dangerous Drugs, which required signatories to set up agencies to monitor and investigate illicit drug trafficking.

By 1930, the United States had its own enforcement agency in the form of the Federal Bureau of Narcotics, whose commissioner, Harry J. Anslinger, became a driving force shaping both his own national and the international narcotics agenda up to his retirement in 1962. Anslinger, who had served in the US State Department before becoming cssistant commissioner of the Bureau of Prohibition, waged an implacable campaign against drugs, emphasising a supposed nexus between drug consumption and violent criminality. He opposed drugs education on the grounds that this was tantamount to encouraging consumption and insisted that withdrawal of drugs was the only acceptable treatment for addiction. A skilled and cynical bureaucrat who manipulated statistics on consumption and arrests to sustain and bolster the status of his bureau, Anslinger is best known in the US for launching a one-man crusade against marijuana, a drug he variously portrayed, on the basis of no real evidence, as promoting violence and as a gateway drug which initiated the user to stronger substances.[6] In doing so he used language notably devoid of political correctness but characteristic of the era, a typical example being 'Reefer [sic] make darkies think they're as good as white men'.[7] Anslinger's assault on marijuana was to prove a significant complicating factor in subsequent narcotics-control policies, taking up increasing amounts of law-enforcement attention and arguably detracting from a greater focus on those drugs responsible for the greatest harms. Notwithstanding the US's disengagement from the League of Nations, Anslinger was active in promoting his stark and uncompromising prohibitionist approach to drugs in the international arena, exploiting the desire by League of Nations member states for greater US engagement and developing bilateral counter-narcotics relationships with 22 countries, enabling narcotics traffickers to be extradited to the US.[8]

Internationally, Anslinger's star came into the ascendant during and after the Second World War. He was largely responsible for ensuring that the League of Nations' counter-narcotics offices were relocated to the US following the outbreak of hostilities in Europe, and he exploited his control of America's near-monopoly stockpile of opiate-based painkillers during the war as a way to extend his international influence. As the prospect of eventual victory over the Axis powers became evident, Anslinger focused on replacing the existing international narcotics-control regime with arrangements more in line with his philosophy, beginning by extracting a commitment from the UK and the Netherlands to end their colonial opium monopolies once the war was over. Though far from a straightforward or linear process, the efforts of Anslinger and a group of like-minded prohibitionists culminated in the 1961 Single Convention on Narcotic Drugs, so called because it replaced nine previous international treaties dealing with narcotics control (see Appendix I for the key details of the 1961 convention, the 1971 Convention on Psychotropic Substances and the 1988 Convention against Illicit Traffic in Narcotic Drugs and Psychotropic Substances, which collectively form the bedrock of international legislation of narcotics control).

The 1961 convention represented a compromise between competing interest groups – primarily, traditional growers of poppy and coca who sought to avoid a blanket ban on agricultural production; manufacturing states in Western Europe whose main concern was to avoid a ban on the production and sale of manufactured drugs; and user states who felt threatened by drugs and espoused maximalist positions on narcotics control.[9] But overall it marked a consolidation of the prohibitionist approach, with the emphasis very much on curtailing agricultural supply, despite lifting an earlier restriction on the number of states able to cultivate opiates for licit medical purposes. The convention encouraged states to enact domestic legislation criminalising all aspects of the production, sale and possession of illicit narcotics, to which category marijuana was added. The existing system of two schedules for classifying drugs according to perceived harms was expanded to four. In due course, the 1961 convention was supplemented by the 1971 Convention on Psychotropic Substances, the main aim of which was to bring manufactured and synthetic drugs such as LSD and amphetamines into the global prohibition regime, something industrialised states had previously resisted on the spurious grounds that such products were both inherently superior and supposedly non-addictive. The 1988 convention regulated the international trade in precursor chemicals and made provisions to combat the laundering of the proceeds of illicit trafficking and international trafficking per se. It also required signatory states to legislate domestically to criminalise the possession of drugs for personal consumption (an issue on which the 1961 convention had been unclear), but with the proviso that a regime of 'treatment, education, aftercare, rehabilitation or social reintegration of the offender' may be a substitute for criminal prosecution.[10] Though the 1961 convention left many gaps in the global prohibition regime, the two subsequent conventions, combined with a succession of ad hoc amendments and the national legislation which the international treaties required, resulted in a significant tightening of the global prohibition system.

Responsibility for operationalising the terms of the conventions was and remains primarily with signatory states. But with the new conventions came new international organisations and processes responsible for overseeing the arrangements enshrined in the conventions. In 1968 the Permanent Central Opium Board (PCOB) gave way to the International Narcotics Control Board (INCB), reflecting the much wider range of illicit substances the new regime was intended to police. The board consists of 13 members, three of whom are required to have relevant medical or pharmaceutical experience, who are appointed for five-year terms by the UN Economic and Social Commission (ECOSOC). Members are expected to conduct their activities independently of national governments. The INCB has three main responsibilities:

- administering the system of global estimates to ensure adequate supplies for licit scientific and medical use of substances controlled under the conventions;
- monitoring the control system for precursor chemicals used to produce controlled substances; and
- monitoring the efforts of governments and international organisations to ensure that the provisions of the conventions are adequately implemented and where necessary recommend remedial measures.

The INCB has in recent years attracted some criticism for conducting its activities in excessive secrecy – no records of the INCB's deliberations are made public, which the INCB argues is necessary to preserve its independence – and for acting, as former UNDCP Chief of Demand Reduction Cindy Fazey alleged, not just as guardians of the conventions, but also as interpreters of them in ways going well beyond their remit.[11] It is certainly the case that the INCB has tended towards a purist interpretation of the conventions in respect of issues such as the UK government's decision to downgrade cannabis from Class B to Class C – a decision which was subsequently reversed. The same approach has been applied to clean needle and syringe programmes (NSPs) implemented by a number of consumer countries with the aim of reducing blood-borne infections such as HIV/AIDS among addict communities. The UNODC has accepted that such programmes are treaty-compliant, but INCB continues to express reservations[12]. Political oversight of the INCB is exercised through the Commission on Narcotics Drugs, an annual gathering of all signatory states in Vienna which discusses issues related to global drug-control systems and also the work programme of the INCB and the main UN agency for drugs control, until 1998 the United Nations Drugs Control Programme (UNDCP) and now the United Nations Organisation for Drugs and Crime (UNODC).

As mentioned earlier, UNODC has become the primary source of information on the global drugs trade but also undertakes a range of technical cooperation projects in member states and provides normative assistance with domestic counter-narcotics legislation. The UNODC purports to adopt a disinterested approach to this work, but it has been argued that, because it depends on voluntary contributions for 90% of its funding, with many of these contributions earmarked by the donors for specific projects, it has found itself obliged to focus excessively on supply-reduction issues rather than on demand-reduction issues of drug-abuse prevention and public health. There have also been inconsistencies of emphasis as between the UNODC and other UN agencies such as the United Nations Development Programme (UNDP), the World Health Organisation (WHO) and the World Bank in circumstances where the supply-reduction agenda runs counter to economic development and human-rights considerations. While constrained by the demands of key donor countries, the UNODC, in its 2008 World Drugs Report, made something of a departure from orthodoxy by calling on signatories to the conventions to treat drug addiction as a public-health rather than a criminal-justice problem. But that seems to have been driven primarily by outgoing Executive Director Antonio Maria Costa seeing his departure (in 2010) as his only chance to tell it the way he saw it. Since then UNODC has reverted to a more orthodox prohibition-based approach.

The 1961 Single Convention came into being at a time when global consumption of illicit narcotics was at an all time low. As mentioned in an earlier chapter, cocaine had fallen out of fashion by the late 1920s and levels of consumption were minimal. A total opium ban by China, the lack of which had bedevilled international efforts to curb opium production and consumption for the first half of the twentieth century, cut consumption levels by over 80%, aided by the ending of colonial opium monopolies in other parts of East Asia. The impact of the latter was offset to some degree by an increase in opium production on the Shan plateau in Burma and in the highlands of Laos by anti-communist insurgent groups. But levels of addiction in consumer countries until well into the 1960s were minimal. In 1945 the US's opiate addict population was just 20,000, rising to 68,000 by 1969, to which must be added an estimated 81,000 users and addicts serving in the US military in Vietnam. By 1973, the total had risen to 559,000 as an anti-establishment counter-culture which took hold in the US and parts of Western Europe fuelled a major expansion in the use of a wide variety of psychoactive substances.[13]

In response to rising public concern about levels of addiction among Vietnam veterans, President Richard M. Nixon launched a series of initiatives which collectively have been characterised as America's 'War on Drugs'. Nixon's motives appear to have been mixed, combining a genuine abhorrence of psychoactive substances and fear of societal breakdown associated with their use with awareness that an agenda of being tough on drugs and crime could be a vote-winner.

Nixon has since been cast in the role of lead villain by all those opposing past and current US counter-narcotics policies. But his 1971 Special Message to the Congress on Drug Abuse Prevention and Control was far from being a clarion call to arms. Although in the accompanying press statement Nixon characterised drugs as 'public enemy number one', the statement to Congress strikes a careful balance between supply- and demand-reduction and makes clear that the bulk of the additional US$155m of emergency funding requested by Nixon to address this problem would go to newly established federal demand-reduction and drug-treatment programmes.[14] Above all, Nixon's statement reflected the need for a fragmented and uncoordinated approach to narcotics to be brought together in a coherent and focused national policy. The same is true of his 1973 message on the establishment of the Drug Enforcement Administration (DEA) as a replacement for several previous organisations, in which he stated in terms that his administration had 'declared an all-out global war on the drug menace'.[15]

Internationally, the focus of Nixon's War on Drugs was Turkey which, via the French Connection, supplied 80% of the US market (the Turkish opium used in the French Connection was overspill from a licit medical production programme). By 1973 a combination of diplomatic pressure and the provision of US$35m in economic assistance had persuaded Turkey to end opium production. At the same time, Franco-US law-enforcement collaboration led to the arrest of the main protagonists of the French Connection. The preliminary results appeared to vindicate the Nixon approach: practically overnight, the price of heroin in New York tripled and purity levels declined. The number of US addicts had fallen from 500,000 in 1975 to 200,000 by the end of the decade. But as heroin consumption in the US fell, it increased commensurately in Western Europe, fuelled by new sources of supply from Southeast Asia.

By 1980, Western Europe had between 190,000 and 330,000 heroin addicts; in the Netherlands alone, the number of addicts rose from 100 in 1970 to 10,000 a decade later.[16]

The US policies of the 1970s appear in retrospect to have witnessed the start of a dynamic resulting in a diversification of sources of supply, smuggling routes and consumption choices for hardcore drugs users. With Turkish production closed down, heroin production migrated first to Southeast Asia – the Golden Triangle – then to South and Central Asia – the Golden Crescent – with the former subsequently re-emerging as a major supply centre following its recovery from a prolonged period of drought in 1978. Meanwhile Mexican criminals responded to the DEA's success in interdicting heroin from Southeast Asia by supplying US markets with a markedly inferior type grown and refined in Mexico, a phenomenon which was in due course to be replicated in Colombia during the 1990s. As Alfred McCoy has observed,

> by the late 1970s the simplex of the Turkey–Marseilles–New York heroin pipeline had been replaced by a complex of international smuggling routes that tied the disparate zones of First World consumption to Third World narcotics production. With production and consumption now dispersed around the globe, the international traffic was far more resistant to suppression than ever before.[17]

A further unanticipated consequence of the US approach was a propensity by user communities to resort increasingly to poly-drug use. As the supply of one drug dried up, users would simply begin consuming another substance, or to the use of multiple substances simultaneously, an example being the 'speedball' – a highly dangerous mixture of cocaine and heroin taken intravenously – which became popular in the US in the 1980s. In the US, cocaine took over from heroin in the 1980s, first as the 'white collar' drug on which President Ronald Reagan declared war in the early 1980s,[18] then in the form of crack cocaine which devastated inner-city communities and led President George H.W. Bush to declare a similar campaign.[19] Western Europe lagged about a decade behind the US: heroin was the predominant problem drug until the 1990s, when cocaine began to take over. In the 1990s, the US again witnessed a significant increase in the consumption of heroin in a smokeable form – only possible at relatively high levels of purity – which had none of the negative social connotations associated with 'mainlining'. Nor of course has the choice solely been between these two drugs; others, notably methamphetamines and cannabis, have also featured, as has alcohol.

More importantly, US counter-narcotics rhetoric was not always matched by reality. In a security climate dominated by the Cold War, counter-narcotics not only failed to attract the level of resources that might have achieved some traction on the problem but also fell victim on occasion to the dictates of realpolitik. During the later stages of the Vietnam War, a task force of DEA agents in Bangkok was seeking to interdict heroin refined from opium transported to Bangkok by Air America under the aegis of the CIA, this being the price the US had to pay to engage the services of Vang Pao's Hmong guerrillas against the Vietcong. During the 1980s, the status of Panamanian President Manuel Noriega as a key US ally in a region convulsed by ideologically driven violence meant that the US had to tolerate his involvement in cocaine smuggling until it was able to overthrow him in 1989 in *Operation Just Cause*. Similarly, for a brief period in the 1980s, the CIA was obliged to look the other way while the Contras funded themselves via cocaine shipments to Miami. This is not to accuse

US policymakers of cynicism; their overall intent in respect of suppressing narcotics was always clear. It is rather to recognise the hard and often unpalatable choices that are the reality of policymaking.

A more valid criticism of US counter-narcotics policies was that very quickly the focus of effort shifted away from demand management towards a supply-management agenda almost exclusively concentrated on the hard-security dimensions of eradication, interdiction and arrest – what some commentators have referred to as the securitisation of counter-narcotics.[20] It is certainly true that, of the counter-narcotics assistance provided to foreign states, itself a fraction of total US counter-narcotics spending, the bulk has tended to be in the form of military or security assistance- either capacity building of indigenous forces or eradication. In the case of Colombia, 75% of US assistance between 2000 and 2005 – amounting in total to US$3.8bn – was devoted to the military component. In the same period the Colombian government spent US$6.9bn on counter-narcotics, half of which was for military or security capacities.[21] However, it should be borne in mind that much of the expenditure over this period was driven less by the counter-narcotics agenda per se than by the perception that Colombia, an important ally of the US, appeared to confront the risk of state collapse as a consequence of narcotics-enabled violence.

And with the carrot of financial assistance came the stick in the form of the threat of de-certification, a variant on the long-established US practice of using the granting or withholding of Most Favoured Nation (MFN) status as a policy lever. Under this process, first applied in 1986 but based on legislation enacted in 1961, the US president was required to submit to Congress an annual determination of the level of counter-narcotics cooperation of major narcotics-producing and transit states. Failure to meet the criteria resulted in de-certification,

which could translate into reduction of aid budgets and opposition by the US government to the approval of loans from
multilateral institutions. In practice, de-certification has been
used only sparingly and mostly against pariah states such as
Afghanistan and Myanmar during a period when their international isolation meant that the economic consequences of
this process were negligible. In many cases – Peru, Bolivia,
Paraguay, Haiti, Cambodia and Nigeria – de-certification
has been waived on national-security grounds. Even Hugo
Chávez's Venezuela, de-certified in 2005 on the basis that it
has repudiated all counter-narcotics cooperation with the
US, continues to receive US financial assistance to promote
democratisation. And although the threat of de-certification
may have galvanised some governments to take action against
the drugs trade, as has arguably been the case with Bolivia,
Mexico and Colombia, it is far from clear that the results have
justified the political ill-feeling the process has generated. Nor
have attempts to sugar the pill, through trade agreements
designed to diversify narcotics-dependent economies, had the
desired effect. In 1991, the US Congress approved the Andean
Trade Preference Act (ATPA) – which subsequently morphed
into the Andean Trade preference Extension Act (ATPEA) – to
promote economic diversification and reduce dependence on
coca-growing. But the impact of the act was significantly atten-
uated as a result of US domestic political lobbying, which led
to the exclusion of many commodities, including tuna, sugar,
footwear, textiles and petroleum, which provided significant
income streams for Andean countries.[22]

At a domestic level the War on Drugs has translated into
an approach which prioritises criminalisation over treatment
and rehabilitation, a phenomenon particularly though not
uniquely evident in the US. Since the 1970s, the US prison
population has risen fourfold to 2.3m, with a further 5m on

parole or probation.[23] Roughly a quarter of all prisoners have been incarcerated for non-violent narcotics-related offences, often simple possession – although this figure must be treated with caution, since at least some of those sentences may have been the result of plea bargaining down from more serious offences. Moreover, the reasons for the US's high prison population go well beyond the issue of counter-narcotics. An equally if not more important driver has been the prevalence since the 1970s of supply-side approaches to criminology, based on the proposition that an environment in which high numbers of ethnic-minority youths grow up in single-parent families would automatically translate into a need for significant investment in additional correctional facilities.[24] Other political and cultural factors have probably also contributed to the US's uniquely high levels of incarceration.[25] But of the US$40bn allocated to domestic counter-narcotics programmes at federal and state levels, 75% is devoted to apprehending and incarcerating dealers – often small-time retailers – and users. Only one-sixth of total federal counter-narcotics expenditure is devoted to treatment and rehabilitation, a far cry from the model envisaged by Nixon.

Elsewhere in the world, the picture is more complex. Some states have counter-narcotics legislation which is more draconian that anything in the US penal code. There is a mandatory death penalty for the possession of relatively small quantities of narcotics in Malaysia, for example.[26] In Western Europe, the general trend has been away from incarceration for simple possession towards a greater focus on treatment regimes – an approach which the 1988 convention explicitly countenances. Some countries have wholly or partially decriminalised the possession for personal use of some drugs, predominantly marijuana, including 12 states within the US where marijuana, though technically still illegal, can be prescribed for medical purposes.[27] The most widely cited example of this approach is that of Portugal which, since 2001, has adopted a policy of decriminalisation of possession of all drugs for personal use, combined with mandatory treatment and rehabilitation programmes and the continued criminalisation of trafficking. The significance of the Portuguese experience will be considered later.

For all the efforts made at a national and international level to constrain the supply of drugs through eradication, interdiction and criminal prosecutions, global levels of drug use have remained stubbornly high. In 1998, the United Nations Drug Control Programme (UNDCP) launched an initiative for the elimination of all illicit coca and opium poppy by 2008 with the strapline 'A Drug-free World'. The mechanism for the launch was a United Nations General Assembly Special Session (UNGASS 1998). Though UNGASS sought to strike a balance between supply- and demand-reduction, the focus of UNGASS 1998 remained heavily loaded in favour of supply reduction. And, as Peter Reuter and Franz Trautmann have observed, 'The global drugs problem clearly did not get better during the UNGASS period. For some countries (mostly rich ones) the problem declined but for others (mostly developing or transitional) it increased, in some cases sharply or substantially'.[28] Despite this judgement, a review conference conducted by UNODC in March 2009 effectively endorsed the aims of UNGASS 1998 and extended the programme for another decade.

In its 2008 World Drugs Report, which reviewed a century of drug controls, UNODC listed five unintended consequences of the global prohibition regime. These were:

- the creation of criminal black markets;
- policy displacement, by which is meant the propensity

of a law-enforcement approach to crowd out the public-health dimension of counter-narcotics;

- geographical displacement, otherwise known as the 'balloon effect', whereby pressure on narcotics production in one location simply leads to it moving elsewhere;
- substance displacement, whereby consumers move from one drug to another depending on fluctuations in availability and price; and
- the social exclusion and marginalisation of drug users.[29]

The 2008 report was quite far reaching in terms of advocating a shift away from existing practices, but amounted to little more than a case for a course correction rather than the fundamental change of course away from prohibition for which some had hoped. It did not consider what alternative options there might be or whether these different approaches could stand a more realistic chance of improvement upon the status quo.

CHAPTER THREE

The producer states

Colombia

Colombia's experience over the past 40 years offers a para-digm of the impact that illegal narcotics trade can have on national and human security. Colombia's difficult geography has always militated against the establishment of a strong, centralised government, even in the pre-Columbian period (pre-1492); the country's recent history has been character-ised by high levels of political violence that long pre-dated its emergence as a global centre for cocaine production. Indeed, until the 1970s little coca was grown there; most cultivation took place in neighbouring Peru and Bolivia, where coca leaf had traditionally been chewed as a mild stimulant, appetite suppressant and means of combating altitude sickness. Nor had there been much global demand for cocaine as a recrea-tional drug. Recreational cocaine use was briefly popular in the US in the 1920s but fell out of fashion in favour of ampheta-mines as its harmful effects and addictive properties came to be more widely appreciated.[1]

By the 1970s, cocaine came back into vogue in the US as a recreational drug of the affluent. At this time, it received little

attention from a US government whose focus was on suppressing imports of heroin from Southeast Asia and marijuana from
Latin America and the Caribbean. Pressure on the marijuana
trade in Mexico and Jamaica led to both a corresponding
increase in cultivation in Colombia and to a move by Colombian
traffickers to take over wholesale distribution within the US
from Cuban gangs. As cultivation shifted to Colombia, so too
did US pressure on the Colombian government to crack down
on the trade. In response, Colombian traffickers increasingly
moved into cocaine, which had the benefits of being less bulky
and odorous than marijuana – hence easier to smuggle – and
offered much higher returns. Initially, the main Colombian role
was in turning coca base from Peru and Bolivia into cocaine
in covert laboratories. But the inexorable business logic of risk
reduction led to increased coca cultivation within Colombia
itself.[2]

A number of economic and social factors contributed to a
dramatic upsurge in demand for cocaine in the US and the
incentive and ability of Colombian traffickers to meet this
demand. Within the US, the collapse of traditional labour-
intensive heavy industry during the 1970s devastated the
economic and social structures of many inner-city neighbourhoods. Creating and servicing a market for drugs in these
neighbourhoods, especially for crack cocaine,[3] was one way in
which poorly educated and otherwise unemployable young
men could earn a living and acquire some social status. For
their part, the drugs offered solace to many who saw no hope
of turning their lives around. By 1985, it is estimated that
some 5.8m Americans had become regular crack users.[4] At the
same time, within Colombia a process of rapid urbanisation
was taking place. Initially, manufacturing was able to absorb
the shift, but increased competition from Asia in areas such
as textiles soon resulted in large-scale urban unemployment.

Meanwhile, the consolidation of agricultural land ownership in ever fewer hands drove many of those who remained in the countryside to migrate southeast into the jungle plains, which increasingly became the principal region of coca cultivation.

The growing cocaine trade led to the emergence of a first generation of powerful, vertically integrated cartels based in Medellin and Cali, whose activities covered all aspects of production, distribution and the laundering of what quickly became immense proceeds from the trade. The operation of these cartels was characterised by a combination of organisational sophistication and brutality. In addition to creating their own intelligence services and armies of professional assassins (*sicarios*), the cartels hired lawyers, accountants, actuaries and MBAs to manage the different aspects of their business. They spent significant sums penetrating Colombia's law enforcement and judiciary, whose members were offered the now familiar choice of *plata o plomo* – money or death. Efforts were also made to influence the political process, with cartel funding of successive presidential candidates an open secret. Two leading cartel members, Pablo Escobar and Carlos Lehder, even entered politics themselves: Lehder set up his own short-lived political party, the Movimiento Civico Latino Nacional (MCLN). The leaders of the Medellin and Cali cartels also made substantial investments in local community projects such as social housing, churches, schools, hospitals and sports complexes and effectively became the main source of employment in both cities. But despite this generosity, the leaders of the cartels found their business so lucrative that they had difficulty disposing of the proceeds. Total cartel earnings by the late 1980s were estimated at US$6bn, of which between $3bn and 4bn were profits.[5] Escobar's personal fortune was estimated by the 1989 edition of *Forbes* magazine at US$9bn and a 2009 book written by his brother Roberto offers a graphic account of the sheer physical difficulties the brothers experienced in dealing with so much hard cash.[6]

The high degree of economic prosperity and social stability generated by the cartels, however, came at a price. The *sicarios* of the Medellin cartel were notorious for their brutality and inventiveness – to say nothing of the rate at which they disposed of rivals. By 1988 the city was experiencing a homicide every three hours. Frustrated by their inability to gain acceptance by Colombia's traditional elite and increasingly threatened by the prospect of extradition to the US, the cartel bosses appeared less than invulnerable to state action. The Colombian government's decision to sign an extradition treaty in 1987 gave rise to a massive increase in violence, which involved the Medellin cartel under Pablo Escobar mounting a full-frontal armed challenge to the state. They carried out bombings, kidnappings and assassinations, including that of the minister who signed the extradition agreement with the US. Eventually, after a brief period of extremely luxurious incarceration in a Colombian jail cell built to his own specifications and from which he continued to run his business empire, Escobar was hunted down and killed in 1993 by the Colombian police, with significant assistance from the US law enforcement, military and intelligence agencies, under direction from a government that was now treating cocaine as a serious problem.[7]

The demise of the Medellin cartel, far from ending the problem of organised narco-trafficking in Colombia, simply transferred it to a much larger number of what have been termed micro or boutique cartels, such as the Norte del Valle cartel headed by individuals such as Wilbur Varela and Carlos Montoya. The term micro-cartel hardly does justice to organisations that were still enormously powerful, wealthy, well organised and able to subvert the Colombian state through a combination of corruption and intimidation. The captured records of Norte del Valle kingpin Juan Carlos Ramirez Abadía (aka *Chupeta*, or lollipop) indicated that in 2004 he alone was responsible for exporting 122 metric tonnes of cocaine, scarcely a boutique quantity.[8] But these smaller cartels had learnt the key lesson of Pablo Escobar's demise and avoided posing a direct armed challenge to the government's authority. They also, over time, moved from a vertically integrated model dominating all aspects of production and supply towards a model characterised by greater flexibility and specialisation, which saw the supply routes to the US gradually move to the control of the Mexican cartels. Since the turn of the millennium, a series of increasingly sophisticated police and intelligence operations enabled by financial and technical assistance from the US and the UK has resulted in the decapitation of successive iterations of micro-cartel leadership, giving rise to a further process of fragmentation. Nonetheless, this had not of itself had any impact on levels of supply from Colombia.

But the increasingly serious threat to the stability of the Colombian state posed by the Medellin cartel was quickly superceded by a far more serious threat in the shape of the Fuerzas Armadas Revolucionarias de Colombia – Ejercito del Pueblo (FARC-EP, hereinafter referred to by the more widely known acronym FARC). FARC was one of a number of left-wing insurgent movements which arose out of a prolonged period of political violence known in Colombia as La Violencia, which is generally assumed to have been sparked by the assassination in 1948 of Liberal presidential candidate Jorge Eliecer Gaitan Ayala and which pitted supporters of the Liberal Party against the Conservatives. La Violencia was a product of enormous dissatisfaction with a political system which saw economic and political power concentrated in the hands of a wealthy land-holding elite. Much of the violence took place in rural areas where the state had never established a convincing presence and in which public order, such as it was, was maintained by private militias. The human-security implications of La Violencia were enormous: between 200,000 and 300,000 deaths, three to four times as many injuries and over one million internally displaced persons (IDPs)[9] created the conditions for what was to become an endemic pattern of rural violence and injustice.

Formally established in 1966 and rather reluctantly adopted by the orthodox Marxist Communist Party of Colombia as its military arm, FARC initially seemed a strategically irrelevant anachronism, its repertoire limited to undertaking periodic ambushes of Colombian armed forces in the remote jungle areas of central Colombia, where it maintained a precarious foothold. It was not until 1982, at its Seventh Conference, that FARC articulated and began to implement a strategy that was to take it, by the late 1990s, to a point where it posed an existential threat to the Colombian state.[10] FARC needed to increase its force levels and weaponry to implement a Maoist strategy of taking control of the countryside and surrounding the cities. And in order to do so, it needed to raise revenues. At first ideologically hostile to the coca cultivation, FARC's approach to the narcotics trade evolved from an initial policy of imposing a 15% tax – *gramaje* – on coca production in areas under its control towards what eventually became engagement in all facets of the trade. By 2002, FARC's annual earnings from drugs were thought to be in the region of US$140m.[11]

FARC's engagement in the cocaine trade coincided with a significant increase in coca cultivation within Colombia itself, driven by US pressure on coca production in Peru and Bolivia and increased aerial surveillance, which inhibited flights bringing coca base to Colombia for processing. Trafficking groups took bags of coca seed to the communities which had established themselves in the southeast and south of Colombia. For such communities, located far from major conurbations and lacking transport links, coca cultivation represented a rational choice, given the long production life of the plant. It is naturally pest resistant and requires relatively little work once planted. Once picked, the dried coca leaves are collected at the farm gate, thus obviating all the logistical problems and uncertainties involved in getting other forms of produce to a market where prices may fluctuate in an arbitrary and unpredictable fashion. Many cultivators, however, opt to go the next stage of producing coca base, a simple but messy and environmentally very harmful process involving petroleum and sulphuric acid (one tonne of coca leaf produces between 1kg and 1.5kg of coca base, which can be turned into an equivalent quantity of cocaine). By the late 1990s, Colombia was producing at least 700 tonnes of cocaine per year, almost all of it from coca leaf grown domestically.

Thanks in large part to its growing involvement in coca production and cocaine trafficking, FARC was able to expand from a few hundred operatives to around 16,000 divided into 70 operational fronts covering 40–60% of Colombian territory. Militarily, in a classic 'war of movements', FARC was regularly inflicting defeats on Colombian security forces, which lacked both the training and resources to deal with such a threat and which had initially relied on right-wing rural militias to counter FARC. These militias, many of which ultimately coalesced into the Autodefensas Unidas de Colombia (AUC), were themselves deeply implicated in the cocaine trade and other criminal activities and were responsible for significant human-rights abuses, including the forcible displacement of large numbers of peasant farmers. By 1998 the overall security situation in Colombia had deteriorated to the point where road travel out of Bogota, as well as Cali and Medellin to mention a few, was almost certain to result in either death or kidnapping, and Western governments were beginning to speculate that Colombia might be heading towards state failure amid a perfect storm of narcotics-enabled violence.

In retrospect, it is clear that 1998 represented FARC's military apogee, as the Colombian army, which by then was receiving much-enhanced military training and technical assistance from the US, was able to attack FARC's fixed positions from the air. This change actually pre-dated Plan Colombia, an initiative agreed by presidents Andres Pastrana and Bill Clinton in 2000. The plan provided for a significant injection of US funding for the Colombian army and police to undertake counter-narcotics activities, including aerial eradication. Plan Colombia was in fact agreed during a period of peace negotiations with FARC under which the group was accorded a demilitarised zone – *zona de despeje* – in their heartland regions of Caqueta and Putumayo, which accounted for some 200 tonnes of Colombia's annual cocaine production.[12] In the face of mounting evidence that FARC was not sincere about peace negotiations and was using them as a strategic pause to regroup and re-arm, Pastrana revoked the *zona de despeje* in February 2002, just five months before fulfilling his term in office. Shortly afterwards, his replacement Alvaro Uribe inaugurated the Plan Patriota, in its essence a classic counter-insurgency 'clear, hold, build' strategy designed to drive FARC and other insurgent groups to the margins of the state and to establish institutions and governance where none had previously existed. (The two initiatives ran side-by-side for a time, often drawing funds from the same source, which partly explains why the latter is mistakenly referred to as a successor for the former.[13])

Plan Colombia had originally been conceived by Pastrana as a comprehensive social and economic strategy designed to wean Colombia's peasantry off coca cultivation. Pastrana explained: 'Drugs are a social problem whose solution must pass through the solution to the armed conflict ... Developed countries should help us to implement as sort of "Marshall Plan" for Colombia which will allow us to develop government investments in the social field, in order to offer our peasants different alternatives to the illicit crop.'[14] In the event over 80% of all foreign assistance, almost all of which came from the US, was devoted to developing Colombia's hard-security capabilities. And although formally the assistance was provided for counter-narcotics, in practice it became increasingly difficult to distinguish between the capabilities devoted to counter-narcotics and counter-insurgency, reflecting the reality that both issues intersected with FARC.[15] (There has been much discussion about the extent to which FARC's involvement in the narcotics trade had comprehensively subverted the organisation's original revolutionary purpose. While this may in practice have been true of some field commanders, the evidence from the Reyes archive depicts an organisation whose leadership remained dedicated to achieving power in Colombia by military means, with narcotics revenues seen simply as a means to that end.[16]) Total US investment in Plan Colombia between 2000 and 2008 has been estimated at US$6bn.[17] Over and above this assistance, Colombia's own national-defence budget went from 3.9% of GDP in 1999, peaking in 2009 at 5.1% of GDP before dropping in 2010 to 4.5%, still one of the world's highest.[18] This figure incorporates the budgets of the Colombian National Police, a paramilitary national gendarmerie of 161,655 (as of October 2011) which has played a vital counter-insurgency role.[19]

The results of this high level of expenditure on military and security capabilities have been broadly positive in restoring something resembling normality in a country which had come close to meltdown. During the middle years of the past decade, Colombia's security forces have achieved dramatic progress in combating FARC, whose number have roughly halved to around 8,000 and whose presence has been largely restricted to remote border areas. The 'hold and build' aspects of Plan Patriota are now visible in municipalities such as La Macarena, a former FARC stronghold which is now coca free and policed by the state – though there is some scepticism as to whether this model can be replicated across the country. A number of FARC's senior leaders have been killed, including, in November 2011, their top leader Alfonso Cano; and seizures of FARC documentation from the computers of FARC Secretariat members Raul Reyes and 'Mono' Jojoy have provided important intelligence insights.[20] FARC is now increasingly dependent on cross-border bases in Venezuela, but even these may be coming under pressure thanks to embarrassing revelations in 2010 regarding the nature of Venezuelan government complicity with FARC since the late 1990s. Not all the Colombian government's successes can be attributed solely to increases in numbers and firepower. Enhanced intelligence capabilities, including much improved sharing between the Army and the National Police, and a better system of integrated intelligence assessments, have played an important part. The sophistication of operations such as the 2008 *Operacion Jaque,* in which FARC was deceived into releasing most of its high-value hostages in the mistaken belief that they were simply being transferred from one operational front to another is testimony to Colombian competence in this area. So too is the operation leading to the death of FARC leader Alfonso Cano in 2011.[21]

President Juan Manuel Santos (formerly defence minister in the Uribe administration), who took office in September 2010, has sought to move away from his predecessor's focus on security towards a post-conflict agenda, with the emphasis on economic development, job creation and poverty eradication. But with FARC still unwilling to countenance peace talks and continuing to launch attacks against Colombian security forces and energy installations, the country cannot yet be considered in a fully post-conflict situation. Meanwhile, the Santos administration has to deal with a massive legacy of security related issues amid recognition that the Colombia's security establishment has probably grown beyond sustainable levels. He must also deal with between 3.5m and 4m internally displaced persons, the restitution of 7m hectares of land whose original owners have been forcibly displaced, the re-integration into society of over 50,000 former combatants and the problem of 8m Colombians still living in abject poverty.[22] Under the Victims and Land Restitution Bill enacted by Santos on 10 June 2011, US$25billion has been allocated over ten years. At the same time, as many as 10,000 former right-wing (AUC) paramilitaries who were demobilised between 2004 and 2006 have reverted to criminality, forming what the Colombian National Police have taken to calling BACRIM – *bandas criminales emergentes* (emergent criminal groups). Such groups remain engaged in cocaine trafficking but have also emerged as global players in areas such as people trafficking and currency counterfeiting,[23] and have re-established a culture of violence and extensive human-rights violations in cities such as Medellin.[24] And this is before the detrimental impact of a multi-year conflict on Colombia's economic development is factored in. Apart from the need to maintain a defence budget far above global averages, the opportunity cost to Colombia's economic development of more than 30 years of narcotics-enabled conflict has been estimated at between 2% and 3% of GDP per year.[25] Based on these estimated figures, Colombia's economy could have been between 75% and 125% larger than it currently is.

In terms of its main objective, which was to re-establish security throughout the country and move narcotics-related violence from a national-security to a law-enforcement issue, the Colombian government has undoubtedly met with considerable success, notwithstanding the problems listed above. But if the aim was to eradicate the drugs trade, claims of success are much less convincing. It is certainly the case that cocaine production in Colombia has fallen from a high of 680 tonnes per year in 2004–05 to an estimated 410 tonnes in 2009. While doubts remain about the accuracy of estimates, it is thought that the area of cultivation has fallen to 68,000 hectares.[26] But there has been a corresponding rise in Peruvian cocaine production from a 2000 low of 141 tonnes to 302 in 2009, suggesting what has been referred to as the 'balloon effect', whereby pressure on production in one location simply displaces it elsewhere.

The spraying of glyphosates has been enthusiastically promoted by the US as a solution which reduces coca cultivation and hence the economic base sustaining FARC. The evidence for the efficacy of aerial eradication in reducing the size of the cocaine trade is at best mixed and early claims of significant achievements have to be seen in the context of the civil servants being attracted to simple solutions that offer politicians the comfort of hard numbers, which can then be cited as evidence of success. Moreover, the nature of coca cultivation in Colombia has shifted from large monoculture plantations to one of intercropping with coca bush and subsistence crops, making aerial spraying harder to justify, even if some of the claims about the human harms inflicted by glyphosates prove unfounded.[27] Coca farmers have shown themselves adaptive and resilient in dealing with the effects of spraying, whether by washing the leaves or cutting the bushes back to the stem, enabling them to regrow whilst also developing new strains of coca bush able to produce higher concentrations of alkaloids, translating into smaller and more easily concealed plantations.

Aerial eradication seems set to continue as an article of faith, but thinking in Colombia has increasing moved in favour of taking action higher up the value chain. Dr Daniel Mejia of the University of the Andes argues that spraying one hectare of coca – a costly undertaking given the infrastructure required – removes only US$400 from the value chain, whereas destroying a cocaine laboratory – which is relatively cheap to do – removes US$500,000 plus US$25,000 per kilogram of cocaine destroyed.[28] The need to rethink the focus of interdiction resources has been accepted by the Colombian government and incorporated into a number of policy documents since 2003, the latest being the 2011 Defence and Security Policy, with the aim of attacking the profits of the drugs trade.[29] More emphasis will also be given to greater regional co-ordination in the area of interdiction. Given that US financial assistance to Colombia will in the future be much reduced, it is clearly in the interests of the Colombian government to focus on how to get the best bang for what will increasingly be their own buck.

Afghanistan

The cost to Colombia of fighting the War on Drugs has been, and continues to be, high. But at no point did the domestic value of the drugs trade equate to more than 8% of Colombia's GDP, and that figure has now fallen to somewhere between 1.5% and 2%.[30] In the case of Afghanistan, however, the domestic value of the heroin trade equated in 2007 to 48% of GDP, falling two years later to 26%. For Tajikistan, a key transit state for heroin which is still recovering from the effects of a civil war, the corresponding figure is 30%.[31] Opium cultivation and production has become an economic mainstay of many of the key power brokers on whose support the Karzai administration depends for its continued survival. The drugs trade also makes a significant contribution to fuelling Afghanistan's continuing insurgency with the Afghan Taliban estimated to earn US$125m per year from the trade.[32] The origins of the drugs trade in Afghanistan, which are rooted in that country's experience of almost uninterrupted warfare over the past 30 years, serve as another paradigm of the way in which narcotics production and chronic instability can feed off each other.

Since the overthrow of the Taliban regime in 2001, Afghanistan has become a virtual monopoly producer of the world's opium and heroin supplies. According to UNODC, Afghanistan accounts for 66% of total poppy cultivation and 85% of global heroin and morphine production.[33] The disparity between total cultivation and total production can be explained by the fact that Afghan opium poppy offers significantly higher yields, by a factor of nearly five, over that cultivated in Myanmar, due to differences of climate and soil.[34] Again according to UNODC, in 2007 Afghan opium production peaked at 8,200 metric tonnes before dropping in 2009 to 6,900 metric tonnes and in 2010 to 4000 metric tonnes, the latter drop attributable predominantly to a widespread blight.[35] In 2011, opium production bounced back to 5,800 metric tonnes. Total heroin production in 2009 was 548 metric tonnes (opium converts to heroin at a ratio of roughly ten to one but a proportion of opium is consumed in unrefined form).[36] The global value of the opium trade has been put at US$65bn, of which US$55bn is accounted for by heroin and morphine.[37]

The two biggest single markets for Afghan heroin are Western Europe, whose 1.6m addicts are estimated by UNODC to consume 88 metric tonnes per year, and Russia, whose 1.5m addicts account for 70 metric tonnes. Heroin is trafficked from Afghanistan by a multiplicity of routes with no single organisation or ethnic group in a dominant position, in a combination of bulk consignments and small quantities. The main flows are to Russia via the so-called Northern Route through the Central Asian states of Tajikistan and Uzbekistan, with indigenous groups fulfilling demand from Russian organised criminal groups. Some of this enters Eastern Europe. The so-called Balkan Route sees heroin transiting Iran, itself now plagued by a growing problem of heroin abuse, often in heavily armed multi-vehicle convoys, thence to Turkey and the former Yugoslavia. Again, no single trafficking group predominates, though the largest trafficking groups are either Turkish/Kurdish or Albanian. The Southern route involves transportation of bulk consignments of heroin through the Baluch desert of Pakistan to the Makran coast, whence it is shipped westwards. The enormous variety of methods whereby heroin is trafficked testifies to the low obstructability of narcotics, making them uniquely attractive to a wide range of actors. Due to the fact that much heroin is smuggled in small consignments, UNODC estimates that trafficking may employ up to one million people.

Opium poppies have always been cultivated in Afghanistan. By the 1930s Afghanistan was recorded as producing 75 metric tonnes of opium per year, of which a significant proportion was for domestic consumption. But in the 1970s a combination of factors gave rise to a significant increase in opium cultivation in Afghanistan: these included the imposition of bans on opium cultivation in Iran and Pakistan and a combination of drought and political instability which led to a reduction in supply from Southeast Asia's Golden Triangle. A more important catalyst, however, was the Soviet invasion of Afghanistan in 1979 and the emergence of an indigenous resistance movement – the mujahadeen – which benefitted from significant financial and logistic support from Pakistan, the US and Saudi Arabia. A number of mujahadeen leaders from the Pashto-dominated south of the country, including Gulbuddin Hekmatyar, leader of the Hezb-i-Islami group, and Mullah Nasim Akhundzade, a Helmand-based commander of the Harakat-e-Inqilab-e-Islami, began to supplement their foreign subventions by involvement in the opium trade. Akhundzade in particular was well placed to exploit the agricultural potential unleashed during the 1950s and 1960s by US engineers associated with the Helmand Valley Authority, a massive irrigation project modelled on the Tennessee Valley Authority. He set up a system whereby farmers were given an annual quota of opium to produce and threatened with beatings or castration if they failed to deliver. From that point onwards, Helmand has been the centre of Afghan opium-poppy cultivation accounting in 2010 for 57% of total production.[38]

The Soviet approach to counter-narcotics was of a piece with their approach to counter-insurgency operations generally, with a heavy emphasis on a scorched-earth policy which destroyed many of the country's traditional irrigation channels; rendered much agricultural land unusable, due to the widespread dispersal of anti-personnel mines; and led to the displacement of some 5m Afghans, a third of the population. The Soviet departure led to a civil war, followed by a period of warlordism in which many military commanders derived benefit from the opium trade in the form of taxation, various forms of protection or direct involvement in production. Agricultural production during that period was adversely affected by a prolonged drought which forced many farmers to resort to opium cultivation. Opium poppies are hardier and more drought resistant than other crops (although yields from irrigated land are unsurprisingly much higher) and the farm-gate prices much higher than potential alternative crops. These factors are to some extent offset by the fact that opium cultivation requires six times more man-days per hectare than wheat. When the Taliban, a group of mainly Pashto graduates of Deobandi madrassas in Pakistan, took power in 1996 with significant Pakistani logistic support and financing from Saudi Arabia, Afghanistan was producing 2,248 metric tonnes of opium per year. By 1999 this figure had risen to 4,565 metric tonnes, before dropping drastically to 186 metric tonnes in 2001, reflecting a total ban on opium production imposed the previous year.[39]

The Taliban decision to permit opium cultivation, notwithstanding the clear position in Islam that such activities are *haram* – unlawful – was driven by pragmatism, in particular the need to secure the consent of significant populations in the south of the country who for the reasons outlined above had become dependent on poppy cultivation. The revenue earned from taxation of opium production also provided a valuable supplement to funding from Saudi Arabia and wealthy individuals in the Gulf states. Traffickers thrived under the rough and ready but effective security regime established by the Taliban, which included a system of single tolls for roads, replacing the multiple and arbitrary tolls previously exacted by local warlords. By 2001 large-scale operators such as Haji Juma Khan Baloch controlled large laboratory complexes in areas such as the well-watered Chagai Hills on the border with Pakistan. From these laboratories, bulk consignments of heroin were transported in heavily armed convoys of up to 150 vehicles across the Balochistan desert to Pakistan's coast for onward shipment by boat or aircraft.

The overthrown of the Taliban in 2001 by the US and its allies was achieved largely by engaging the help of a disparate collection of warlords and tribal leaders, many of whom had been displaced by the regime. Some US$70m was disbursed as an incentive either to displace the Taliban from the areas formerly controlled by the warlords or to guarantee that they would not be able to return there. The warlords went on to form an important component of the government of President Hamid Karzai at both national and regional level. As James Cockayne and Daniel Pfister have observed, this set the scene for the evolution of much of Afghanistan's post-conflict economic and social evolution.

> When local warlords were incorporated into the early state-building efforts … they gained enlarged freedom to participate in organised crime … The result is a very significant illicit economy which undermines human security throughout the country, fosters corruption, decreases state tax revenues, destabilises the local currency, encourages market speculation and infla-tion, crowds out investment in the licit economy and increasingly forces large sections of the population into the illicit economy in the search for access to credit and a reliable income.[40]

Meanwhile, the post-conflict reconstruction efforts of the international community were plagued by a combination of unrealistic expectations, inadequate resources relative to these expectations and a lack of cohesion and clarity as to objectives. Much of the aid effort was focused on what donors thought Afghanistan needed, with little consideration given to the wishes of the intended recipients or the cultural context. Under Donald Rumsfeld, the US Department of Defense was notori-ously resistant to involvement in state-building, and in any case the US military quickly became distracted by the need to plan and execute the invasion of Iraq. Many NATO coalition partners in Afghanistan were subject to an array of national caveats which imposed constraints on their deployability. To the embarrassment of the coalition, opium production in Afghanistan quickly began to skyrocket, with many of the Afghan warlords now in government acting, in Barnett Rubin's words, as 'powerful new protectors' of the opium trade[41] – protection being the area where most money was to be made.

From the first, there was a serious tension within the international community as regards the relative priorities of counter-insurgency (COIN) and counter-narcotics. The main concern of NATO/ISAF, whose numbers were not remotely close to those needed to impose effective security, was to ensure popular consent for their presence and activities and a muscular approach to counter-narcotics was seen as incompatible with that objective. In the early days of the ISAF mission it was, for example, not unheard of for lorries loaded with opium to be waved through military check-points. This situation changed somewhat in 2005 when, under pressure from a US Congress concerned by reports of rising opium production, counter-narcotics was reluctantly adopted as part of the US military mission.[42] But the military approach remained unenthusiastic and reactive. As late as 2006 Supreme Allied Commander Europe (SACEUR) General James L. Jones was quoted as saying that he agreed with those who did not see counter-narcotics as a military mission. And it was only in October 2008 that a NATO ministerial meeting determined that a prohibition on ISAF taking direct military action against narcotics traffickers and laboratories should be overturned.[43] Notwithstanding this decision, some NATO/ISAF partners, notably Germany, retained a national caveat on counter-narcotics activity.

Under the terms of the United Nations Assistance Mission to Afghanistan (UNAMA), set up in 2002 to oversee Afghan state reconstruction, the UK was accorded the international lead on counter-narcotics with the aim of reducing cultivation by 70% over five years. Once the enormity of this task began to dawn within Whitehall, desperate efforts were set in train to deliver short-term, verifiable progress. Practically overnight, a plan was put together for a compensated eradication scheme whereby farmers would be paid a sum for each *jerib* (a fifth of a hectare) of poppy destroyed. After one year the scheme was quietly abandoned in the face of problems of verification – some farmers took the money but didn't eradicate – and evidence both that much of the money had been diverted by the local officials through whom it was channelled and that the scheme actually constituted a perverse incentive for additional opium cultivation. Thereafter the UK's main contribution to counter-narcotics came via the creation of the Afghan Special Narcotic Force (ASNF). The ASNF had some effect by virtue of its ability to project a visible Afghan national government presence where previously none had been evident, and was able to persuade local communities in some areas to abandon poppy cultivation. But its main role was in carrying out interdictions higher up the value chain, a task made somewhat easier once the UK government had established a system of narcotics courts and a prison where those arrested might be securely held – though few traffickers of any consequence have seen the inside of this facility, thanks to a deeply entrenched culture of impunity.

Opium eradication efforts combined both carrot and stick. The carrot came in the form of crop-substitution policies – so-called alternative livelihoods – seen by many Western policymakers as the incentive which would persuade farmers away from poppy cultivation. But efforts to introduce such programmes suffered from being both sporadic and under-resourced, with the lack of an effective nationwide microcredit scheme being a major drawback. Alternative livelihoods also failed to acknowledge one of the key realities of Afghan poppy cultivation. As David MacDonald has put it:

> Throughout Afghanistan, opium has become a non-perishable, low-weight, high-value product that represents a commodity to be exchanged, not only for the purchase of food but as the means of achieving

food security, providing the resource poor with access
to land for agricultural production and credit during
times of food scarcity. In a country with few secure
financial institutions, basically it acts as the family's
bank.[44]

Indeed, a better analogy might be to see opium as a social-
security system, enabling Afghan farmers to see themselves
through lean times such as droughts, or to meet contingencies
such as medical emergencies or the provision of dowries for
children. While farmers in areas of relatively high security,
with access to roads and reliable markets, might well have
seen the benefits of moving to other cash crops, most Afghan
farmers were not in this situation and needed to hedge their
bets. They also needed to achieve a modus vivendi with local
warlords, whose interests were also a major factor in determining the scope of poppy cultivation in the areas they controlled
and against whom they could secure no protection.

Some of these warlords, now rebadged as senior provincial officials, also engaged in forced eradication when it suited
their interests. In many cases these consisted of sabotaging
cultivation by potential rivals, as was the case in 2003 with the
eradication programme launched by the governor of Helmand,
Sher Muhammad Akhundzada. Other Afghan officials took
substantial bribes not to eradicate poppy. Against this it should
be noted that there were some examples of genuine bans being
successfully imposed, such as in Nangahar province. And
opium cultivation in the north of the country, where there was
both greater stability and more economic opportunities, underwent a substantial decline. In 2008, the US government, under
pressure from Congress and unimpressed at the perceived
paucity of the UK's efforts, undertook programmes of forcible
eradication using local Afghan eradicators trained and directed

by the US contractor DynCorp.[45] A year later, in the face of extensive rioting by the farmers whose fields were targeted, resulting in a number of deaths, these (expensive) efforts were abandoned.[46]

US attention then turned to aerial eradication, drawing on the experience of Colombia. This approach overlooked the significant differences between the two cases; in Colombia, the targets of aerial eradication were in the main large monoculture coca plantations in remote and largely uninhabited jungle areas, whereas in Afghanistan most poppy is grown around human settlements and intercropped with other agricultural produce. The potential for loss of consent was enormous and objections by President Karzai, discreetly encouraged by the British, eventually translated into a formal ban on aerial eradication in 2005, something which successive US ambassadors to Kabul have sought to overturn. Only in 2009 did the Obama administration take a policy decision to move away from mass eradication in favour of a more focused policy of alternative livelihoods. But pressure continued from other quarters. At a NATO–Russia Council meeting in March 2010 a demand by Federal Narcotics Service Director Viktor Ivanov for NATO/ISAF to undertake large-scale eradication – a figure of 25% was suggested – was rejected.[47]

By 2005, a re-invigorated insurgency directed out of Quetta in Pakistan by the Afghan Taliban leadership, assisted by groups such as the Haqqani network and Pakistani tribal groups who were to coalesce in 2006 into the Tehrik-i-Taliban-Pakistan (TTP), pushed the counternarcotics agenda further onto the back burner for the US military and its NATO/ISAF allies. Until 2006, when an UK battlegroup deployed to Helmand (*Operation Herrick*), there had been a minimal military presence in the Pashto heartland areas, in the case of Helmand a 150-strong US military contingent forming part of a Provincial Reconstruction

Team (PRT), based at Lashkar Gah, whose activities had posed no threats to either opium traffickers or insurgents, who had until that point been free to operate with few constraints. Until his replacement was insisted upon by the UK, Helmand governor Sher Mohamad Akhundzada had effectively presided over a narco-economy, as evidenced by the discovery of nine tonnes of opium in the basement of his residence immediately prior to his removal.[48] Indicative of the prevailing culture of impunity was the fact that Akhundzada was given a ministerial position, subsequently becoming a senator.

The insertion of the British forces, followed by a Dutch deployment to Uruzgan and a Canadian deployment to Kandahar in 2006, was akin to thrusting a stick into a hornets' nest. The ensuing escalation of violence has been written about extensively and it would be otiose to recount it in detail. During the first fighting season, NATO/ISAF forces found themselves ranged against significant concentrations of insurgents in what initially resembled a conventional conflict, but which over time morphed into a more familiar model with the insurgents increasingly relying on asymmetric tactics, in particular the use of improvised explosive devices (IEDs).[49] NATO/ISAF forces were too few to hold territory taken from the Taliban, and the Afghan National Army (ANA) and police were not up to the task. Indeed the Afghan police, many of whom were untrained and illiterate, created more problems than they solved through a predatory approach which alienated local populations, driving them further into the arms of the Taliban. The situation was further exacerbated by a six-month pattern of military *roulements* which resulted in a lack of strategic cohesion and continuity with each new commander effectively devising and implementing his own strategy. By 2009 NATO/ISAF casualties were mounting against a backdrop of growing opposition within NATO countries to a war whose purpose no longer seemed clear and which NATO/ISAF did not appear to be winning.

This certainly was the view taken by General Stanley McChrystal, when in the summer of 2009 he was tasked by US Defense Secretary Robert Gates to produce an Initial Assessment Report of the counter-insurgency campaign. The report, dated 30 August 2009 and leaked to the *Washington Post*, characterised the situation in Afghanistan as 'serious' and 'deteriorating'. McChrystal concluded that 'failure to gain the initiative and reverse insurgent momentum in the near term (12 months) … risks an outcome where defeating the insurgency is no longer possible'.[50] McChrystal identified four elements in the campaign that needed to change: firstly, NATO/ISAF had to extend efforts to increase responsive and accountable governance; secondly, the Afghan Security Forces – police and army – had to be expanded to 400,000; thirdly, Afghanistan had to be viewed as a single theatre of operations; and finally, there needed to be clear interaction with the local population.

In November 2011, US President Barack Obama announced in a speech at West Point that an additional 31,000 troops would be sent to Afghanistan as part of a surge designed to help reverse the deterioration. Under General McChrystal and then subsequently General David Petraeus, a conventional counter-insurgency (COIN) strategy was implemented with a focus for the first time on the 'hold' and 'build' strands of a campaign conducted under a unified US command. Plans were put in place significantly to increase the numbers of Afghan National Security Forces (ANSF) to 296,000 in June 2011 and a projected 305,000 by October 2011, under a combined NATO Training Mission – Afghanistan (NMT-A) – and a US Combined Security Transition Command, Afghanistan (CSTC-A).[51] A process of transition from NATI/ISAF to Afghan security control was begun with most of Kabul, the provinces of Bamiyan and

Panjshir and the cities of Herat, Lashkar Gah, Mehterlan and Mazar-e-Sharif passing to Afghan control in July 2011.[52] A combination of intelligence-led raids by special forces began to substantially erode the number of mid-ranking insurgency commanders and significant progress was made in restoring normality to former insurgent strongholds in Helmand and Kandahar provinces.

The achievements of NATO/ISAF since late 2009 cannot be underestimated. But there remain serious doubts about whether a full transition to Afghan security control by the projected date of 2014, announced as the date on which US combat troops are expected to be withdrawn from Afghanistan, will be achievable. Nor is it clear how easily a state whose total GDP in 2010 was estimated at US$15.61bn[53] will be able to sustain security forces whose cost is estimated at US$6bn per year,[54] at a time when Western enthusiasm for funding the Afghan project is bound to have waned. Meanwhile, NATO/ISAF's achievements on the battlefield came at a cost; since the 2001 US invasion, total deaths in Afghanistan are estimated at around 40,000, of which just over 2,500 are NATO/ISAF forces. And with the Taliban and its allies unable to prevail on the battlefield, their focus increasingly has turned to asymmetric attacks in which most victims are civilians. In March 2011, the head of the Afghan office of the International Committee of the Red Cross (ICRC) issued a report which said that 'the first two months of 2011 have seen a dramatic deterioration in the security situation for ordinary Afghans' to the point where their lives had been rendered 'untenable'.[55]

A key element in the recommendations arising out of McChrystal's assessment report was the need to focus on improved governance, with a particular focus on combating the endemic problem of corruption. Launching a report entitled 'Corruption in Afghanistan: Bribery as Reported by its

Victims' at the International institute for Strategic Studies on 19 January 2010, UNODC Director Antonio Maria Costa observed that 'drugs and bribes are the two largest income generators in Afghanistan: together they correspond to about half the country's (licit) income'. The UNODC report was concerned with the phenomenon of bribery at a retail level and the impact this was having on levels of consent for the Karzai administration. But at a macro level, the figures and their implications were even more alarming. If opiates were what primed the pump of top-level corruption, what kept the motor running was huge Western, and in particular US, aid budgets disbursed with scant regard for the absorptive capacity of a shattered state and with little accountability or oversight. It is estimated that, between 2007 and 2010, US$3bn was smuggled out of Afghanistan in the form of hard cash, mainly to the Gulf states.[56] In 2010 it was discovered that the Kabul Bank had lost US$910m of its investors' money in unrecovered insider loans to bank shareholders, threatening a collapse of the Afghan banking sector.[57] A senior ISAF official characterised the Afghan Air Force, established with US funding, as 'an ISAF-enabled international smuggling ring'.[58]

Meanwhile for the Taliban and its allies, profits from the opium trade continued to constitute a significant component of their overall income, estimated variously at 20–50%. Taliban commanders often operated opium banks, with deposits and withdrawals being made according to circumstances. But it is debatable whether the continuing insurgency was dependent on opium revenue to the point where a serious assault on the opium trade – assuming such a thing could be managed – would seriously degrade the insurgents' capacity to continue fighting. The Taliban and their allies derived revenue from a variety of other sources: various forms of smuggling, kidnapping, donations from wealthy supporters in the Gulf and

Saudi Arabia and property investment in Dubai, where most commanders will typically have a trusted relative based in order to manage their portfolios. From 2010 onwards, NATO/ISAF began to speak of the need to integrate counter-narcotics into the military campaign, but with a focus on intelligence-led interdictions and prosecutions higher up the value chain which can be made to stick.

Afghanistan's future is clouded by considerable uncertainty. The US and its allies are showing clear signs of war weariness amid much questioning within domestic constituencies about whether the current COIN campaign is either necessary or affordable. As indicated above, a plan for a security transition to the Afghan government, to be accompanied by an end to US and allied combat operations and corresponding troop withdrawals by 2014, has been set in motion.[59] The hope is that by that point, the Taliban and its allies will have been sufficiently pressured by the reinvigorated NATO/ISAF campaign to have a serious interest in peace negotiations. Preparatory talks were apparently already taking place in 2011 between the US government and representatives of the Taliban's leadership in exile, the Quetta Shura. The expectation is that, whatever the outcome in 2014, the US will seek to retain significant military capabilities in Afghanistan – though that outcome is not guaranteed in the face of sustained pressure from neighbouring states. It is also assumed that its allies will retain commitments to continue various forms of development assistance, though how durable those commitments will prove in an era of financial stringency remains unclear. Meanwhile, there is little to indicate that Afghan standards of governance will be significantly better by 2014, and there are some grounds for thinking they may actually deteriorate, as powerful individuals stockpile resources against an uncertain future. Continued violence is almost a given, the best hope being that the government in Kabul will by that point have amassed enough power and resources, combined with some continued measure of Western support, to withstand any security challenge whilst confronting limits on its ability to project power across the country.[60]

The future for opium cultivation in Afghanistan looks equally unclear. Opium cultivation has developed as a survival response in conditions of insecurity and the absence of circumstances within which a licit economy can develop. But over the past decade the opium trade has become vertically integrated into the Afghan economy to a point where powerful vested interests militate against its eradication. In circumstances where Western economic assistance to Afghanistan seems bound to diminish and alternatives such as the exploitation of Afghanistan's significant mineral wealth may be slow to materialise, it is hard to imagine opium playing a lesser role in Afghanistan's economy for some time to come. Consumer countries would be well advised to plan on the basis of that expectation.

Conclusion

Colombia and Afghanistan are self-evidently very different countries with very different historical experiences. But since the 1970s, both have suffered from massive levels of violence which were enabled and perpetuated by the global trade in illicit narcotics. In Colombia's case this violence came close to posing an existential threat to the state. And in Afghanistan's case that threat was realised. The violence took place within a wider geopolitical context of East–West confrontation which significantly complicated and aggravated the situation confronted by each state. This ideological factor remains a driver for continuing violence in Colombia.

The response of the international community, and in particular of narcotics-consuming countries whose demand for drugs has fuelled both the trade and its attendant violence, has been different in each case. Colombia, a country always closely aligned ideologically with the United States, has been able to attract sufficient political and material support from successive US administrations – and to a much lesser degree from the United Kingdom – to hold the line against both criminal gangs and insurgent groups and to stage a fight-back which has brought a significant measure of stability as well as much enhanced prospects for economic development and the promotion of social justice. But drugs-related criminality and an insurgency which, though ideologically driven, is fuelled by drugs revenues, remain serious preoccupations inhibiting Colombia's ability to move to a post-conflict agenda and to address the long legacy of social and economic damage. The risk of a slide back into greater levels of violence cannot be excluded. And any progress in reducing the quantities of cocaine produced in Colombia has been more than compensated by an increase in production elsewhere in Latin America, notably Peru.

Having allowed Afghanistan, in words attributed to British politician Sir Geoffrey Howe, to lapse back into the obscurity whence it came following the end of the Soviet occupation, the attention of the international community was wrenched back there following the 11 September 2011 attacks on the US, planned and orchestrated out of Afghanistan by Osama bin Laden. Opium cultivation, always present to a limited degree, blossomed into a major accelerant of violence as a pragmatic response by Afghan peasant farmers to the absence of state institutions. Since the US invasion of Afghanistan in late 2001, the US and its allies have tried without success to resolve the conundrum of how to fight a counter-insurgency campaign while also bearing down on what is close to being a monopoly supply of the world demand for illicit heroin and opium. The reality, as argued by Vanda Felbab-Brown in her book *Shooting Up*, is that the objectives of these two campaigns are irreconcilable, and that restoring security is a necessary prelude to conducting effective counter-narcotics operations. The prospect of this sequence being realised in Afghanistan is remote; both the Afghan government and the insurgents rely heavily on revenues from the opium and heroin trades. It is hard to envisage a peaceful future for Afghanistan and equally hard to contemplate a future in which Afghanistan does not provide the bulk of global heroin supplies.

Notwithstanding the harm done in consumer societies by cocaine and heroin – much of which is a function of the fact that these drugs are illegal – this pales into insignificance compared to the harm inflicted on producer states, as evidenced by the two examples above. This disparity of impact is an ineluctable consequence of an international control regime, which has placed a disproportionate emphasis on supply while relegating demand-control to the province of law enforcement.

CHAPTER FOUR

The transit regions

The negative impact of the narcotics trade on transit countries and regions is arguably as great – if not greater – than on producer states. Mexico, Central America and West Africa all serve as key transit points in global narcotics trafficking. Analysis of these geographically disparate areas illustrates numerous parallels in the way that the narcotics trade affects the security, governance and economic-development prospects of transit states, even though the ways in which these insecurities manifest themselves are specific to each region.

Mexico

Drugs clearly have a significant impact on Mexican society, when one considers the plight of 1,500 Mexican cities that are currently infiltrated by cartels. Approximately 450,000 people are involved in the cultivation and trafficking of narcotics, the illicit market for which is estimated at $14 billion per year (marijuana: $8.5bn; cocaine: $3.9bn; methamphetamines: $1bn; heroin: $400million).[1]

Mexico has a long history of illicit drug trafficking dating back to the 1910s, when it first became established as a major producer and trafficker of narcotics for the US market. By the 1930s, production of opium poppy and marijuana had boomed. Mexico had become an attractive tourist destination for Americans seeking to indulge in activities that were illegal in the US, and local entrepreneurs and politicians were determined to seize this financial opportunity in spite of the fact that all exports of heroin and marijuana had been declared illegal in 1928. With US legislative and enforcement efforts focused on combating cocaine and heroin, Mexican criminals concentrated their efforts on smuggling marijuana, since the drug had an ambiguous legal status in the US at the time. In the 1930s the country witnessed the beginning of what Monica Serrano has described as a 'local but vertical system of political-criminal relations',[2] whereby local politicians were willing to tolerate – or even support and regulate – certain criminal activities in exchange for bribes and help in subduing political opponents, leading to the establishment of 'elite-exploitative' relations that thrived as power in the Mexican state was, at the time, highly fragmented. While the symptoms of these symbiotic relationships were most evident in the northern states, in 1931 the country experienced its first drug-related national scandal, when the interior minister and the head of Mexico City's police, together with other senior officials, lost their jobs amid allegations of collusion with narco-traffickers.

With the outbreak of the Second World War Mexican opium cultivation received a boost, owing to the reduced access to other opium sources and to a pervasive but unsubstantiated belief that the US would ask Mexico (and Canada) to promote legal cultivation of opium for the production of morphine. This was followed by US efforts to curb growing cultivation through eradication programmes in the north of Mexico. Yet limited funding and suspicion that Mexican Army officers were tolerating or even colluding with opium production and trade meant that limited progress was made and several drug scandals were revealed during the 1940s.[3]

Politically, the country was led by the leftist party Partido Revolucionario Institucional (PRI) for 70 years (until 2000). The Party was formed in the late 1920s with the goal of ending the political unrest that followed the Mexican Revolution (1910–1920). In the late 1940s it assumed its current name, the PRI (having previously been known as Partido Nacional Revolucionario (PNR) and Partido de la Revolución Mexicana (PRM)), and in the 1950s began to assert stronger support for civilian control by eliminating military figures from the party ranks. It also ensured that PRI candidates won local elections, and overall it established a relatively stable authoritarian system. At this time the country had come to the realisation that strategic dependence on the US was the only feasible option and relations between the two countries began to improve following a tense previous decade (Mexicans had accused the US of invading their country on no fewer than 13 occasions). However, behind a stable facade was a narcotics industry directed and regulated by, this time, the central government, with the police and the Direccion Federal de Seguridad (DFS) – the first federal agency responsible for drug control, established by the PRI – in charge of transit points rather than the criminals. In addition, officials stressed the need for keeping levels of violence at a minimum and within certain areas, as well as opposing the creation of an internal market, and not allowing traffickers to hold political positions. These measures were aimed at keeping the growing Mexican middle class and strategic partners happy.

In 1972, Turkey prohibited the export of opium to the US, creating a window of opportunity for Mexican traffickers who went on to secure 80% of the US heroin market within three years, a remarkable increase from their 15% share pre-1971.[4]

The US and Mexico then decided to embark on a joint operation to eradicate opium poppy: 1975 *Operation Condor*. If anything, the operation exposed the level of corruption of Mexican forces and several high-profile arrests were made among police ranks. Even though the Mexican state had portrayed itself as willing to cooperate with Washington on counter-narcotics, it was clear that by the mid-1980s traffickers were still in business and ready to take their activities to the next level.

As discussed in the previous chapter, while Mexicans had been the key players in the opium and marijuana industry in Latin America, Colombian cartels had the leading role in the establishment and development of the cocaine trade. However, as trafficking increased along traditional routes so did US seizures, especially in the Caribbean. For this reason, in the late 1980s Colombian cartels were prompted to seek alternative land and maritime routes through Mexico, and Mexican criminals proved to be the ideal partners in the trafficking business as they had long controlled the smuggling of illicit goods (drugs from Mexico to the US and weapons from the US to Mexico) across the Mexican–US border and had an extensive network within the US. At the same time the Mexican system of state regulation of trafficking had started to erode as cartels increasingly came to dominate in a privatised business model and a number of governmental agencies, including the DFS, were dismantled (with some paramilitaries later joining the cartels as enforcers). The combination of their experience, the fact they were paid in kind for their services, and the decline of the major Colombian cartels in the mid-1990s allowed Mexican cartels to graduate from being couriers on behalf of the Colombians to taking full control of the business, relying on Colombians only as suppliers. As of 2010, US authorities estimate that approximately 90% of cocaine entering America has been transported across the Mexican–US border.[5]

Cartels

Led by Mexico's most wanted drug trafficker Joaquin 'El Chapo' Guzman, the **Sinaloa Cartel** – which first came to notoriety in the 1960s and 1970s as the target of President Nixon's War on Drugs – is thought to be one of the most powerful criminal groups in Mexico. The group has deployed cells in the US and in Nicaragua, El Salvador, Guatemala and more recently Colombia and Peru.

Sinaloa's key competitor, the **Gulf Cartel**, once the most powerful drug syndicate in the country, emerged in the 1970s. The organisation is notorious for its extreme brutality and for the acquisition in the late 1990s and early 2000s of **Los Zetas**, about 30–40 elite army regiment members who had deserted the Special Forces Airmobile Group, one of the most highly trained forces in the Mexican Army. In 2005 Los Zetas, who already possessed military, intelligence and surveillance capabilities, were joined by the Guatemalan Kaibiles, a military force responsible for the massacres that took place during the Guatemalan Civil War (1960–96).[7] In 2010 the Gulf Cartel's leadership started to collapse as a result of infighting, growing law-enforcement pressure under President Calderon's lead, and the arrest of some notable cartel members. The combination of these factors, together with a lack of direction within the group, drove Los Zetas to become an independent force and a player in the drug trafficking scene in its own right.

In 2003, in response to Los Zetas, the Sinaloa Cartel established an armed wing called **Los Negros**, which employed gangs to carry out executions of rival cartel members and police officers. The group, which is now an independent entity, switched allegiances and became the armed wing of the **Beltran Leyva Cartel**, a splinter group of the Sinaloa Cartel, when it came into existence in 2008.

The Sinaloa Cartel was only one of two factions that became established following the split from the original narco-trafficking enterprise in the state of Sinaloa. The other, the **Tijuana Cartel**, was once a key player in the business but is now the least powerful among the cartels. One of its enemies is another historic cartel, in Ciudad Juarez. The **Juarez Cartel** is aligned with the Beltran Leyva Cartel even though its activities do not tend to gain as much prominence.

One of the most recent cartels to have been established is **La Familia**, in 2006. Initially its aim was to defend citizens and fill the security void left by the government. However it soon turned to drug trafficking and to violent executions.[8]

Following years of fighting, in early 2010 the various Mexican cartels formed two competing blocks, one consisting of the Sinaloa, Gulf and La Familia aligned under the umbrella name of La Nueva Federacion, which remains a fairly united block in spite of reports pointing to a possible breakdown of this partnership in early 2011. The second block features the remaining smaller cartels tied together by looser and often changing alliances.[6]

This complex and ever evolving network of alliances, rivalries and brutal violence have deeply affected Mexico over the last 60 years or so. While figures are not available for the pre-President Calderon era, it is estimated that more than 47,000 people had been killed between December 2006 and December 2011 as a result of drug-related violence. More than 750,000 have been internally displaced in the same period.[9]

This criminal network is supported by a number of contractors or junior partners in the form of enforcers, such as Los Negros and Los Zetas, prison gangs such as the Mexican Mafia (*La Eme*) and Barrio Azteca, and street gangs such as 18th Street and Mara Salvatrucha (MS-13), operating in both Mexico and the US. Hierarchical divisions exist and cartels can rely on La Eme and other dominant prison gangs to contract street gangs to distribute drugs on the outside, carry out killings, operate methamphetamine laboratories in the US, smuggle illegal migrants and weapons, and potentially engage in insurgency operations against the police and the judiciary.[10] While gang members are usually coerced into following orders, it is inevitable that cartels are at times unable to exert full control over gang activities, especially when they take place on US soil, and this has resulted in an increase in violence. But the worst violence is perpetrated by groups like Los Zetas within Mexico, where ever more extreme techniques including skinning, beheading and burning victims with acid are used to instil fear

Map 1. **Cartel infiltration and trafficking routes**

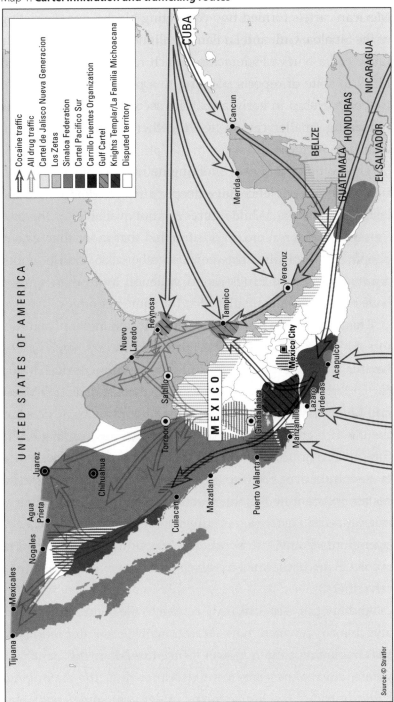

Source: © Stratfor

and respect. Civilians have also been targeted, and the sadistic nature of the violence involved has often been described as 'more akin to terrorist techniques than cartels'.[11]

There is a dichotomy when it comes to propensity to violence between cartels and gangs, especially those based in the northern states. Mexican cartels use violence primarily for financial gain. They belong, according to Robert Bunker and John Sullivan's classification, to the 'phase two cartels' (exemplified by the Cali cartel in Colombia) of 'subtle co-opters' using violence symbolically rather than indiscriminately (as opposed to the 'phase one' type represented by the Medellin cartel).[12] In the case of gangs, violence is more deeply rooted in endemic problems affecting the very social fabric of the country. Lack of education, employment and opportunities in deprived areas is likely to lead young males (and females to a lesser extent) to join gangs. The abundance of weapons and the belief that violence is the only effective response for any real or perceived wrongdoing make these organisations particularly brutal. In addition, unlike cartels, gangs are tactical rather than strategic players, engaged in trying to corrupt or influence government officials. They are less sophisticated and generally less concerned with outcomes beyond the immediate goal of protecting their territory. These characteristics are incorporated in their modus operandi when engaging in drug-related activities as subordinates of the cartels. Illegal immigrants from Central America transiting Mexico en route to the US are kidnapped by gangs for ransom or pressed into their ranks.[13]

Another cause of insecurity relates to the nature of Mexican police forces, which have traditionally been decentralised and fragmented, with power concentrated in the hands of local municipalities and limited authority at the state level. The country's 2,000 police forces underwent some consolidation since 2000, but not enough to address the lack of strong security institutions or the corruption, abuse and ineffectiveness that continue to hinder the establishment of a modern law enforcement apparatus. Presidents Zedillo, Fox and Calderon have all tried to introduce police reforms through various approaches, respectively the militarisation of the federal police; the establishment of professional investigative policing; and the restructuring of the federal police and increased financial investments into the security and justice systems. Mexico's police are now much better trained and equipped, and enjoy better co-ordination between different forces, yet police reform is inevitably a long process, much affected by domestic political considerations. All Mexican police chiefs are political appointees (which often results in patronage appointments), and there is a tendency for new administrations simply to distance themselves from their predecessors by doing something 'different'. Thus reform is hindered by a lack of continuity and by the wasting of considerable time and resources adjusting to new processes.[14] Police forces in Mexico have traditionally been highly susceptible to corruption, especially at the municipal and state level. One of the prime implications of this problem is that municipal and state police, who have no responsibility over drug trafficking as it falls within the federal police jurisdiction, are infiltrated by the cartels and often protect traffickers from federal investigations.[15] Together with the fact that cartels have often possessed greater capabilities than the police, this problem prompted President Calderon to deploy the army as soon as he took office in 2006 to launch an offensive against the cartels, beginning with the deployment of 6,500 troops. A further 35,000 were deployed the following year as part of a progressive increase of resources, which culminated in the deployment of more than 50,000 military personnel against the cartels.[16]

In spite of these efforts, a 2010 poll showed that about 50% of Mexicans felt that security had worsened and only 21% believed that the country had become a safer place under President Calderon, indicating that support for his war on the cartels was in decline.[17] Indeed, statistics show that 2010 witnessed the highest level of cartel-related killings – 15,273 – a 60% increase from the previous year.[18] Mexicans have been losing patience and this is likely to be reflected in the presidential elections scheduled for 1 July 2012. At press, PRI's Enrique Peña Nieto was the leading contender, and even though Calderon and his supporters have argued that a PRI government would equate to a victory for organised crime (referring to the party's history of collusion with the cartels during its 70 years at the head of the country), average citizens may remember the era of relative stability that accompanied PRI rule and cast their votes accordingly.[19] In addition, one should not assume that a PRI administration would put a halt to the current effort against organised crime. The criminal scene in Mexico has evolved over time and cartels are now more sophisticated, engage in wider array of criminal activities and are increasingly transnational. Brokering a long-lasting deal with them would be difficult for any government, owing to the high level of competition and fragmentation that remains among the various groups that comprise the two rival cartel alliances.

It is argued that President Calderon's approach, as well as his predecessor's, has had the unintended consequence of intensifying violence and competition among cartels. The strategic aim during Fox's presidency was to pursue a decapitation process designed to break the cartels into smaller and weaker entities which would no longer pose a threat to national security and could instead be addressed as a law-and-order issue. This strategy has been broadly successful, but has had the effect of making the smaller more fractured cartels emerging from the decapitation process also harder to manage and their violence even less predictable.[20] David Shirk has identified three further side effects of Calderon's approach. Firstly, greater power for the military has led to a degree of conflict in its relation with law enforcement. Secondly, as public security became more militarised, corruption among the military has increased, as has the incidence of human-rights abuses perpetrated by military personnel. Thirdly, the number of desertions from the army – prompted mainly by low salaries, poor working conditions and high levels of personal risk – has risen to 20,000 per year, with some adverse security consequences as trained personnel have defected to the criminal gangs.[21]

The spiralling violence in Mexico prompted the US to provide greater assistance, in the form of the $1.3bn Merida Initiative, a three-year deal struck between President Calderon and President George W. Bush in 2007 which would see the transfer of funds, hardware and training from the US to Mexico. The US was criticised for not delivering all the funds and equipment originally promised and in 2010 President Obama agreed to the extension of the initiative – with what is now known as 'Beyond Merida' – to improve intelligence sharing and cross-border security, strengthen law enforcement and the judiciary, and trace and disrupt cartels' revenues.[22] A welcome addition to the Merida agenda is the goal of addressing the economic and social factors underlying the violence through the implementation of community-development strategies supported by the US Department of State and USAID, and led by Mexico's federal agencies.[23]

But it is not just violence that poses a continuing threat: corruption has had a significant effect on the country, undermining state sovereignty.[24] Collusion between cartels and the government was standard practice and it was only with the decline of the PRI and the election of President Fox in 2000 that large-scale arrests were eventually made. Mexico followed this by signing the United Nations Convention against Corruption in 2003 (ratified in 2005), but corruption remained deeply imbedded in the country's political and social life.[25] Indeed, under Fox's successor President Calderon and in spite of promises of reform, Mexico has slipped down Transparency International's Corruption Perception Index from 72nd place out of 180 countries in 2008 to 100th place in 2011. It obtained a score of 3 out of 10 (where 10 corresponds to 'very clean' and 0 to 'highly corrupt').[26] Former Colombian judge Luz Nagle is adamant corruption has become such an integral part of Mexican society that is now almost indispensible in order to preserve equilibrium for both the political and business systems. Mexico's compromised institutions cannot hope to address the many social symptoms of corruption, such as crime, economic crisis, unemployment and public discontent, while continuing to espouse the very system of corruption that gave rise to and exacerbated such problems.[27] The onus, however, should not only be on Mexico. As Calderon pointed out, it is unlikely that tonnes of cocaine could be trafficked across the Mexican–US border without some level of complicity from US authorities. Indeed, the number of investigations and arrests involving US border officers shows the temptation to accept bribes from drug and human traffickers is too strong for some.[28]

While Mexico has not yet become a kleptocracy, there is potential for the emergence of a parallel state dominated by what Bunker and Sullivan have described as 'phase three' cartels – which arise as a result of chronic corruption and weak institutions – ruling over criminal enclaves and effectively acting in place of the state.[29] The consequence of this has been the emergence of no-go areas, such as in Ciudad Juarez and parts of Michoacan and Tamaulipas states, in which the state exercises no effective presence and the overwhelming majority of crimes go unreported.[30]

Central America

Analysts of counter-narcotics frequently refer to the 'balloon effect', which we have described earlier as the geographic displacement of drug cultivation as a result of counter-narcotics activities in a given region. A more powerful, and more graphic, term has been coined by Bruce Bagley from the University of Miami to describe what is happening in Central America, and more specifically in Guatemala: the 'cockroach effect', which refers to the scattering of drug traffickers from regions where they are targeted by government forces to areas where they can operate more freely. Guatemala – where 98% of crimes are unpunished – has become home to many displaced traffickers.[31] In response to increasing interdictions in Mexico, cartels have also exported their business model to most of Central America, where they rely on local criminals and *marras* who act as subcontractors. In addition, the region has graduated from serving simply as a conduit for supply and has moved into production, as evidenced by the discovery of a Mexican-style cocaine factory in Honduras in March 2011.[32]

What is happening in Central America is not simply Mexican history repeating itself across the continent. Compared to Mexico, Central American countries are at a real disadvantage as they are still emerging from a period of conflict that began in the 1960s. El Salvador, Guatemala, Honduras and Nicaragua were the worst affected by internal fighting which claimed the lives of at least 360,000 people by 1996.[33] The conflicts presented obvious Cold War overtones and were a concern for the US, ever worried over the possible spread of communist forces and threats to American interests, such as the Panama Canal. The main victims were large dispossessed indigenous populations confronted by small oligarchic elites aspiring to control most of the resources of the state. The bloodshed left a legacy of social, economic and political instability, as well as security problems. Nicaragua is the poorest mainland Latin American country; nearly 50% of Guatemala's infant population is chronically malnourished and the average citizen has about four years of schooling; Honduras witnessed a successful military coup in 2009; and El Salvador is still dealing with the psychological scars of the civil war and the 1981 El Mozote massacre in particular.[34]

Cocaine bound for the US has transited the region since the 1970s, but the late 2000s saw a major spike in volumes, in particular those shipped through the Northern Triangle (El Salvador, Guatemala and Honduras). According to the US Department of State the amount of cocaine reaching the US via Central America grew from less than 1% in 2007 to 95% in 2010, reflecting the growing use of land-based routes, short-distance aerial trafficking and littoral maritime trafficking taking place.[35]

This shift means that while Mexico retains its key role as a transit country for drugs (as well as producing some of them), a number of Central American countries are now experiencing high levels of drug-related violence, which is seriously threatening some already fragile states. Countries such as Honduras, Guatemala, El Salvador, Panama and to a lesser extent Nicaragua and Costa Rica, have experienced increasing narcotics-related activity. All but El Salvador were designated as 'major drug transit countries' by President Barack Obama in 2010.[36] The World Bank, in its World Development Report 2011, presented data showing the dramatic rise in homicide rates affecting, to varying degrees, all Central American countries. In two of the countries it mentions, El Salvador and Guatemala (up 101% and 91% respectively since 1999), levels exceeded those witnessed during the countries' civil wars. Honduras has also seen homicides increase by 63% in the same period, also as a direct result of increased drug trafficking operations.[37] It is estimated that around 60% of killings in Central America as a whole are drug-related.[38] Even more telling, Honduras's San Pedro Sula has now replaced Mexico's Ciudad Juarez as the homicide capital of the world (it is also the source of two-thirds of the country's GDP).[39]

The impact of such violence on the socio-economic development of these countries is considerable. The World Bank has calculated that 'for every three years a country is affected by major violence ... Poverty reduction lags behind by 2.7 percentage points.'[40] The level of violence certainly shows no sign of abating, given that the value added to criminal revenues by using Central America to traffic cocaine amounts to 5% of the region's GDP.[41] Such a haul makes traffickers well placed to contest governments' counter-narcotics initiatives. Moreover, with the presence of 700,000 gang members in Central America, national armies and police forces are massively outnumbered.[42] In 2010, Guatemalan President Alvaro Colom admitted that four areas within his country were under the control of drug traffickers and that it would require 15,000 additional police and 10,000 extra soldiers in order to reclaim those lawless pockets.[43] Numbers aside, army and police effectiveness is further reduced by a lack of training and equipment. The US Department of State in its 2011 report on El Salvador points out that the National Civilian Police (PNC) receives inadequate training and funding from the central government. In addition, instances of corruption and collusion with criminal groups are numerous, as are human-rights abuses, which undermine police credibility.[44] In Honduras, capacity for preventing, responding to and investigating crimes is very limited. Again, these problems are caused by lack of manpower, training and financial resources, as well as by widespread corruption.[45]

As already alluded to, an additional by-product of growing violence is the increased militarisation of law enforcement in the region. All Central American countries have boosted their defence budgets and the presidents of countries such as Guatemala, Honduras and El Salvador have followed Calderon's footsteps and resorted to deploying thousands of soldiers to fight organised crime alongside, or instead of, the police. This trend does not represent a novelty for Latin America, nor is it an isolated case (Brazil and Ecuador, to mention two examples, have gone down similar routes). The deployment of military personnel, who are by definition not trained to deal with civilians, has resulted in incidents of human-rights abuse as well as cases of corruption among army ranks as a result of increased powers being granted to the military. In addition, continuous military actions against organised crime are not financially sustainable. For instance, President Colom confirmed that the military operations in the department of Petes, following a massacre attributed to Los Zetas in May 2011, cost the government between $127,000 and $190,000 per day for a state of siege that lasted until mid-August.[46] Beside these more practical points, in places like Guatemala, memories of military atrocities taking place during the 1960–96 Civil War are still vivid among citizens, and civil–military relations remain difficult.

Unlike Mexico, where violence is attributed almost exclusively to the cartels and their enforcers, in Central America the criminal scene in multi-layered, owing to the presence of gangs, well-established mafia-style families and the most recent addition of Mexican cartels. The extent of the relation between cartels and Central American criminals in not fully understood, but experts have suggested that such relationships are stronger in El Salvador and Honduras. Los Zetas and Sinaloa appear to be the most prominent Mexican syndicates operating in the region, with the Gulf Cartel playing a minor role. They have replicated the same fierce competition over trafficking routes normally associated with certain areas of Mexico. In Central America they have found an ideal business environment characterised by corrupt bureaucracies, weak governance, ineffective justice systems, abundant weapons, strategic location and great social inequality, which makes for an easy recruitment ground among disenfranchised youth.[47]

While some local gangs have started working for the cartels as subordinates, other local traffickers have tried to exploit the increasing narcotic business to improve their standing and finances, which has often resulted in violent exchanges with the cartels. In Guatemala, the Lorenzanas, Mendozas and Leones families, who traditionally dominated the market prior to the arrival of the cartels, had managed to maintain a relative equilibrium based on close political ties, the ability to protect citizens from small-scale criminality, and the occasional donations and provision of infrastructure for local communities. The families' activities had historically succeeded in limiting violence and building a social base on which they could rely for intelligence on their competitors and the security forces. But in 2008 the Mendozas and the Lorenzanas allegedly hired Los Zetas against the Leones. After having fulfilled their mission and murdered a prominent member of the Leones, Los Zetas then established themselves in Guatemala, where they are now prominent in the southeast and centre of the country, competing directly with the local syndicates.[48] There are contrasting views on the number of Zetas present in Guatemala, ranging from 100 to 500. Their numbers are reportedly swollen by former Kaibiles (Guatemalan special operations commandos), who have formed links with the Mexican gang. The Kaibiles' elite military training, advanced weaponry and brutality make them so feared that minor groups in Guatemala often claim to have links to the Zetas as a way of gaining credibility.[49]

But violence is not the only problem. The profits generated through the narcotics trade fuel other illicit activities and have allowed the diversification of the criminal business model into racketeering, arms and human smuggling, prostitution, kidnapping for ransom and extortion, as well as the creation of small-scale drug dealing resulting from payments in cocaine given to low-key criminals. This cascading effect produced by drug money also gives traffickers and cartels ever greater power to corrupt, since they can more easily buy political favours and expropriate small land owners as well as acquire portions of natural reserves allocated to indigenous communities, which are then used as warehouses for illicit goods or as improvised landing strips.

The US is monitoring the security situation in Central America closely and has embarked on an assistance programme named Central America Regional Security Initiative (CARSI), originally a part of the Merida Initiative, which includes funding for training and strengthening law enforcement in the region together with refurbishment of patrol boats, aircraft and provision for radios and other equipment used for interdictions. President Obama also launched the Central America Citizen Security Partnership in March 2011 to better co-ordinate donors' efforts in support of the people affected by this wave of insecurity. The World Bank and the Inter-American Development Bank have also pledged to contribute to the project.[50] However, change needs to come from within. The criminal system in place in most of Central America has thrived thanks to 'absent' rather than failing states, as they are often described. Citizens are caught between the government on one side and the criminals on the other. These two actors interact as opponents and, at times, as partners, to the exclusion of the citizens. Perhaps a more important problem in the region is the endemic lack within some of these countries of a political culture in which the state is expected to provide security for its citizenry. Everyone who can afford to do so hires private protection, while the security of the poorest, both physical and financial, is more often than not neglected. For example, in Guatemala, business elites vehemently oppose any security-oriented tax reform, even though the country imposes some of the lowest taxation in the region and the additional income would allow much needed security-sector improvements. Honduras, El Salvador and Costa Rica, meanwhile, have already taken steps to review and temporarily increase taxes to fund security. The absence of security has led to the emergence of several vigilante groups such as Mexico's so-called Mata Zetas, a group of citizens united against the Zetas, perhaps hired by Zetas's rivals. In Guatemala, members of Los Encapuchados have launched a social-cleansing campaign against criminals.[51]

West Africa

West Africa has been a seat of narcotic trade since the first half of the twentieth century, when small marijuana plantations were discovered in Nigeria. In the 1930s colonial authorities started to experiment with growing coca for medical use and at around the same time small shipments of Nigerian marijuana were sent to Europe and the US. In the early 1950s American officials reported that Kano (Nigeria) and Accra (Ghana) were used as transit points by Lebanese syndicates for the movement of heroin from Lebanon to the US. It was only in the 1960s, however, that the West African region started to affirm itself as a major narcotics hub and significant consignments of marijuana were trafficked to the UK. Nigerians, who were in charge of this traffic, were also found in Saudi Arabia, where pilgrimage for the hajj was used as a cover to smuggle cannabis from the early 1970s. A much larger trade emerged in the 1980s, when Nigerian and, to a lesser extent, Ghanaian traffickers began travelling to Latin America and Asia to purchase drugs to be transported back to West Africa before being repackaged and shipped to consumer markets. While consignments were still small, it was at this time that West Africans started settling in producer countries to better coordinate all the phases of the trade. These early traffickers benefited from the fact that European and American authorities focused very little on West Africa, as it was not known as a drug-producing region. This trend came to an end in the mid-1980s when systematic searches of Nigerian passengers became the norm at British airports. At the same time, Nigeria developed a small consumer market, primarily in Lagos, and soon the trade became of interest to politicians and senior military personnel eager to exploit this lucrative opportunity. Nevertheless, while at first narcotics only interested the elites, both in terms of consumption and traffic, the economic decline of the 1980s and the ensuing budgetary cuts and related rise in unemployment prompted a larger section of society to seek alternative forms of livelihood, sometimes illicit. This situation was further exacerbated by the corrupt regime that ruled the country between 1985 and 1993 under General Babangida, making Nigeria an ideal location in which to pursue illegal activities.[52]

Other countries in the region also experienced comparable increases in criminal activities including smuggling of drugs, weapons and diamonds. However, what distinguished Nigerians from their counterparts in, to mention a few, Sierra Leone, Ghana and Burkina Faso, was their level of sophistication, adaptability and entrepreneurial drive. They quickly changed their drug-smuggling routes whenever they came under law-enforcement pressure, established bases both across the African continent and further afield, making connections with other criminal organisations such as the Russian and Sicilian mafias, Lebanese traffickers and South American cartels. By the mid-1990s Nigerian criminals were engaged in bulk shipments of drugs across West Africa.[53] By the end of the decade large shipments of cocaine were seized in West Africa and a growing Latin American presence, especially from Colombia and Venezuela, was evident. This trend can be explained as a result of increased interdiction efforts of the part of the British, Portuguese and Spanish navies, putting pressure on direct transit from Latin America to Europe (especially the Iberian Peninsula), and prompting Latin American traffickers to seek alternatives.

This marked a new phase for West African involvement in the international drug trade, leading to a dramatic increase in cocaine transit through the region. In 2004, drug seizures increased six-fold.[54] Cape Verde, Guinea Bissau and Ghana, to mention a few, were the destinations for large consignments from the Caribbean, Colombia and Venezuela. More than 40 tonnes of cocaine were seized between 2004 and 2005.[55] In West Africa traffickers found extremely fertile grounds due to poverty, high levels of corruption, weak governance and poor law-enforcement capabilities and two main transit hubs were established in Guinea Bissau and Ghana. The geography of some of West Africa's coastal areas provide a safe haven for traffickers: the challenging terrain makes it almost impossible for local authorities to patrol, creating ideal logistic hubs for unloading drugs. Linguistic links, especially in Portuguese-speaking countries; the existence of direct flights from a number of West African airports to Europe; a large Lebanese presence already involved in the narcotics trade; and a well established network pioneered by Nigerian criminals are also factors that draw Latin American traffickers to the region. In addition, while cocaine demand in the US has been in decline for the past two decades, the European cocaine market is growing and presents an alluring business opportunity for Latin American traffickers.[56] Almost all countries in the region are now, to varying degrees, affected by cocaine trafficking and, through cooperation with local criminal groups and Africa-based South American criminals, a number of laboratories have also been created where cocaine is diluted (cut).

With the exception of Nigerian organised criminals, the major criminal actors involved are considered to be less well organised than their Latin American counterparts, but evidence shows that West African criminal networks have become more sophisticated and are expanding their range of operations and activities, such as the production of synthetic drugs, as evidenced by the recovery in 2011 of equipment used for amphetamine-type stimulant (ATS) manufacturing.[57] Dr Kwesi Aning from the Kofi Annan International Peace-Keeping Training Centre in Accra has argued that today's West African groups have become more professional and adopted a non-hierarchical, transaction-based business model whose lack of formal structures and absence of any wider ethnic or family loyalties pose a challenge to law enforcement. Under this model, legitimate businesses are often used as a cover for illicit activities.[58] Europol's 2001 organised-crime threat assessment confirms this assessment. West African groups are listed among the most prominent players in poly-drug trafficking and distribution. They smuggle cocaine, heroin, cannabis and synthetic drugs and have begun to recruit Westerners as drug mules on the basis that they are less likely to attract the attention of customs or law-enforcement officials. Furthermore, they have expanded their trafficking routes.[59] At a UNODC conference in 2011 the head of the West African regional office voiced his concerns that while seizures of cocaine bound for Europe have decreased, this cannot be seen as evidence of successful law enforcement. According to Alexander Schmidt, the reality is that traffickers have simply developed greater sophistication, resulting in decreased rates of detection and interdiction.[60] Similarly another UNODC source stressed that as much as 80 metric tonnes of cocaine, worth $1.2bn, transits West Africa annually and that countries such as Nigeria and Guinea Bissau are becoming prominent transit hubs for Afghan heroin bound for the US.[61]

West African groups have started looking at the region not simply as a transit point, but also as a potential consumer market, leading to an increase in the number of addicts. While statistics for all countries are not available, the UN estimates that about 400 kilograms of heroin were consumed in the first half of 2011 and about 13 metric tonnes of cocaine, with a value of $800m (almost equivalent to Guinea Bissau's GDP) were consumed in the region in 2009.[62] The spread of drug use has a serious impact on society, given the weak public health systems in these countries, and the limited number of rehabilitation facilities. Workers at Remar Ghana, a Christian NGO offering rehabilitation programmes and campaigning to raise awareness on the harms of drugs in schools, prisons and ghettos, confirms that drug abuse is on the rise. Mixtures of cannabis and cocaine – 'cocktails' – are widely smoked by children as young as 12. They also pointed out that, as it often seems to be the case in the region, law enforcement is the first, and often the only, approach used to deal with addicts. At a local prison in Accra in January 2011 (maximum capacity of 700), out of the 3,500 inmates serving their sentences or waiting to begin them, 500 were drug addicts.[63]

Many West African states suffer from corrupt government and poor governance, especially those where predatory governments established themselves following the transition from colonial rule. These governments have often pursued narrow interests that favoured elites, while neglecting the masses. The police and the military have been used as political tools of the regimes, and most institutions deteriorated amid a high degree of corruption. In this context, foreign investments in the legal economy were discouraged and, in some extreme cases, countries hardly had any licit economic sector. The most infamous example of this kind of state is Guinea Bissau, the first narco-state, which relies almost exclusively on agricultural exports and is therefore very vulnerable to criminal infiltration, as evidence shows.[64] Severe poverty and the apparent lack of viable alternatives make criminal activities an attractive way of providing for one's family, as in the case of farmers in Guinea Bissau unloading drug shipments from planes landing on illegal air strips. Moreover, the ability to accumulate wealth, regardless of its origin, may grant political influence and legitimacy; drug barons are sometimes able to provide local communities with services the state is incapable of supplying, which provides them with a degree of public support.[65]

Given the level of corruption that affects a large proportion of the political establishment in the region, the presence of organised criminals does not necessarily translate into instability. Where the ruling elite and organised criminals have a symbiotic relationship, there may be a mutual interest in maintaining the status quo. Of course, conflict between traffickers and the state may arise and violence may follow. Cockayne and Williams share a similar view. They argue that the transit of drugs through the region is unlikely to lead to drug wars. The main threat is posed by the large flow of drug money that has the power to corrupt and erode already weak institutions in developing countries, leading to what they describe as 'junky economies', that is, economies deeply reliant on drug proceeds.[66] These forms of informal economy may be welcome when other economic options are lacking, but they have a long-term effect on the potential for developing strong formal economies. Informal mechanisms, apart from creating the ideal framework for money laundering, run the risk of leading to the establishment of informal governance. This can take the form of enclaves over which the central government has no control, such as in certain areas in northern Côte d'Ivoire or in Accra's slums, and where drug traffickers, rather than the state, provide services for the population. Pointing out examples where this is already occurring, some experts have spoken about the 'Mexicanisation' of West Africa, referring to the power being transferred from the state to the traffickers.[67] This is also a reflection of the low degree of legitimacy enjoyed by most governments in the region, where the population attaches a higher value to the more informal, traditional systems of governance.

It is interesting to note that between 1990 and 1999 Sub-Saharan Africa's GDP per person increased by 15%, and between 2000 and 2008 by 58%. This growth was accompanied by increased imports and exports, a growing middle class and democratic values gaining more prominence. Over the past decade West Africa has experienced the opposite trend. Stability and security have worsened, half of the world's coups have taken place in the region, 60% of people under the age of 25 are unemployed, and organised crime and corruption are rampant.[68] It would be simplistic to point the finger to the narcotics trade as the sole cause of such decline. However, as indicated by the World Bank

> Cross-border insecurity and trafficking, particularly in small arms and drugs, can have highly corrosive impacts on governance and the development of stable, legitimate institutions. Nor are the more fragile states and regions able to counter these challenges

without significant amounts of international help: the resources and manpower available to them can be simply overwhelmed by these non state actors.[69]

Drugs and organised crime can act as accelerants of instability and barriers to development. States such as Ghana, which has registered significant progress towards the achievement of its Millennium Development Goals, risk seeing these gains go into reverse. And states such as Sierra Leone and Liberia, which are emerging out of destructive civil wars, risk a return to high levels of insecurity fuelled by the narcotics trade and drug-enabled corruption. The latter feature would deal a further blow to governance and prevent the state's resources from being used for the good of the people.

Conclusions

The international flow of drugs affects every region it travels through and the case studies discussed in this chapter highlight how serious an impact it has on transit regions. Traffickers are very adaptable and quick to exploit existing weaknesses in the political, economic and security systems of interested regions. Indeed, the expansion of illegal economies thrives thanks to high unemployment rates, corruption, poverty, lack of education and the existence of disenfranchised sections of society. At the same time, illegal networks exacerbate such socio-economic conditions, trapping countries in a vicious cycle of lawlessness and underdevelopment.

The immediate as well as the long-term impacts of this trend have very serious consequences. From an economic point of view, foreign investments would likely generate new local jobs which, in turn, would provide a licit alternative to criminal activities. However, investors are deterred from entering markets in unstable countries where national governments do not appear to have full control over their territory. In addition, owing to involvement in narcotics trade and drug abuse, the very social capital of the countries affected is undermined and the potential for future economic development is seriously threatened, not least because increasing numbers of addicts in drug-transit regions pose a challenge to often basic and under-resourced public-health systems. As a result of limited public-health capacity, treatment for drug addiction is inadequate and often non-existent. It is left in the hands of highly motivated, but equally underfunded, NGOs.

As already alluded to, in all countries affected there are areas where the government has lost its monopoly – including over the use of force – and has been replaced by drug barons and cartel members. In some circumstances this arrangement has unexpectedly resulted in a perverse sort of equilibrium; however, widespread violence among cartels and between cartels and government forces tends to prevail, with the local population being caught in the middle. Taking advantage of the existence of sometimes ineffective security forces, organised criminals have grown stronger and have found an ideal basis for their enterprises. Such cartels have expanded their reach and increased the coordination of their various activities, thereby expanding their impact beyond the boundaries of traditional drug-transit areas, and creating new consumer markets.

CHAPTER FIVE

Alternatives to prohibition

The case studies set out in previous chapters by no means tell the whole story when it comes to detailing the damage to vulnerable societies caused by the drugs trade. An equally valid case study would have been the Caribbean which, though no longer the principal conduit for Latin American cocaine destined for the United States, remains deeply involved in that trade. As a result, the region suffers from an entrenched drugs-fuelled criminal culture which has led to high levels of violence and a proven corrosive effect on national institutions. In 2010, 73 Jamaican civilians were killed in an armed stand-off between government forces and Shower Posse gang boss Christopher 'Dudus' Coke. Coke had previously enjoyed close links with Jamaica's ruling Labour Party, a relationship that disintegrated after the government agreed to extradite him to the US.[1] In mid-2011 the government of Trinidad and Tobago briefly declared a state of emergency to deal with a significant upsurge in drugs-related gang violence.[2] Meanwhile, Brazil's security authorities have struggled to control the influence of drugs gangs in the *favelas* (slums) of major conurbations, many of which have become no-go areas. Further afield, there are signs that the problems associated with West Africa's transit status have begun to migrate to East Africa.[3]

The prohibitionist agenda has resulted in a security-led approach to counter-narcotics, which has become the default approach in the developing world. Confronted with criminal gangs with the resources either to subvert states or to pose a direct challenge to their authority, governments have had to choose between allowing their institutions to be hollowed out by a combination of corruption and intimidation, or to stage a fight-back. In opting for the latter, they invariably set in train a national-security approach to counter-narcotics which inevitably takes precedence over other considerations, such as human security and social and economic development, as resources are focused heavily on the former. This pattern is, to some degree, replicated at the international level, where the UNODC-driven agenda has tended to crowd out the economic development and public-health aspects of drugs policy. Given present circumstances, it is hard to envisage an alternative. But the question arises as to whether there might indeed be feasible alternatives to a prohibition policy and, if so, what the implications of such alternative approaches might be, particularly for the security and stability of fragile and failing states.

Decriminalisation and legalisation

Ethan Nadelmann, executive director of the New York-based non-profit organisation the Drug Policy Alliance, has considered the various viewpoints that contribute to the debate around the approach to drugs:

> Just as 'Repeal Prohibition' became a catchphrase that swept together the diverse objections to (alcohol) Prohibition, so 'Legalise (or Decriminalise) Drugs' has become a catchphrase that means many things to

many people. The policy analyst views legalisation as a model for critically examining the costs and benefits of drug prohibition policies. Libertarians, both civil and economic, view it as a policy alternative that eliminates criminal sanctions on the sale and use of drugs that are costly in terms of both individual liberty and economic freedom. Others see it simply as a means to take the crime out of the drug business. In its broadest terms however legalisation incorporates the many arguments and growing sentiment for de-emphasising our traditional reliance on criminal justice resources to deal with drug abuse and for emphasising instead drug abuse, prevention, treatment and education as well as non-criminal restrictions on the availability and use of psychoactive substances and positive inducements to abstain from drug abuse.[4]

Though Nadelmann's observations would seem to imply that legalisation and decriminalisation are somehow interchangeable, this is not in fact the case. Decriminalisation is the removal of sanctions under the criminal law but with the possibility of imposing administrative sanctions such as fines or compulsory treatment regimes. Decriminalisation normally applies to possession of small quantities of drugs for personal use, though thresholds for determining such use can vary quite markedly between states that pursue this approach. It can be *de jure*, involving changes to the legal framework, or *de facto*, involving the police and other authorities turning a blind eye to breaches of laws which are formally still on the statue books. Perhaps the most informative example of decriminalisation is the regime that has been practised by Portugal since 2001, as it has been in operation long enough for some provisional conclusions to be drawn. Portugal has decriminalised the possession of all drugs for personal consumption, although trafficking in drugs continues to be a criminal offence. Decriminalisation is part of a comprehensive strategy which encompasses prevention, harm reduction, treatment, social reintegration and supply reduction, with those found in possession of drugs being required to undergo treatment and rehabilitation.

A study conducted by Caitlin Elizabeth Hughes and Alex Stevens, which compared trends in drug use in Portugal with neighbouring countries (Spain and Italy) which had not decriminalised drugs, reported the following outcomes:

- small increases in reported illicit drug use among adults;
- reduced illicit drug use among problematic drug users and adolescents, at least since 2003;
- reduced burden of offenders in the criminal justice system;
- increased uptake of drug treatment;
- reduction in opiate-related deaths and infectious diseases;
- increases in the amount of drugs seized by the authorities; and
- reductions in the retail prices of drugs.

Hughes and Stevens manifest an appropriate professional caution in interpreting their evidence, but it does seem to suggest that although the outcome has been mixed, on balance the Portuguese approach has achieved solid success in reducing the most serious health and societal impacts of drug misuse. Also of relevance is the fact that Portugal has not witnessed a significant increase in users from other countries moving to Portugal to take advantage of the more relaxed regime. Nor is there any evidence to suggest that Portugal's policies have led transnational trafficking groups to focus more on Portugal as a trafficking destination.[5] The Portuguese experience goes some way to confirming the results of a 1994 study by C. Peter Rydell and Susan S. Everingham of the Rand Corporation, which conclude that increased expenditure on treatment offers the most cost-effective way to reduce drug consumption as compared with a similar expenditure on eradication, interdiction and domestic enforcement.[6]

The Portuguese example is part of a more general move, at least among Western liberal democracies, away from criminalisation of drugs users to an approach that gives greater focus to public health and rehabilitiation. The administration of US President Barack Obama committed itself to 'restoring balance to US drug-control efforts by co-ordinating an unprecedented government-wide public health and public safety approach to reduce drug use and its consequences'.[7] This initially included the allocation of federal funding for needle and syringe exchange programmes, which were later eliminated as part of a series of negotiations with the Republican Party on budget cuts.[8] Meanwhile, the US State Department has sustained a policy of relentless opposition to 'harm reduction' policies in international forums.

Other states have effectively decriminalised the use of drugs such as marijuana, while in Switzerland and parts of the UK, heroin addicts can receive maintenance dosage treatment. Allowing states to apply the conventions in ways best suited to their specific circumstances seems in principle attractive, in that it may give rise to a greater degree of experimentation, offering better empirical evidence for making drugs policies. Thus far, however, the trend has been towards conformity and a maximalist interpretation of the provisions of the conventions. The scope for experimentation is restricted by the fact that the conventions require all states to criminalise the cultivation, supply and possession of drugs. A 2012 research paper published in the *Lancet* outlined how states wishing to break with orthodoxy and explore more radical policy options must renounce the treaties and then re-apply with reservations – which is easier said than done, given the political pressure likely to ensue from such a move.[9]

But while decriminalisation may have real benefits for consumer societies, it is less easy to see how such an approach can of itself significantly affect the problems of drugs-related insecurity in the producer and transit states of the developed world, at least in the short to medium term. A black market, with all its perverse incentives, continues to exist. If anything, greater competition between criminal groups for shares of a more restricted and hence potentially a more contested market could lead both to increased violence and the creation of incentives to establish new markets in states where none currently exist.

Legalisation is perhaps best expressed in terms of repealing the prohibition of certain goods or behaviours – specifically in this context, the production, supply, possession and use of drugs which are currently prohibited for other than medical purposes. Advocates of legalisation do not specify precisely what policies or legal regimes would replace prohibition, but in general these are seen as involving a significant degree of government regulation, given rise to the use of the alternative formulation 'legalisation and regulation'. The concept is far from a free-for-all, although there are some extreme libertarians who would argue for an absence of all constraints. Serious advocates of legalisation are at pains not to be overly prescriptive, offering instead a range of possible options along the lines of the 2009 publication 'After the War on Drugs: Blueprint for Regulation', by UK drugs policy foundation Transform.[10] But the broad approach advocated is strict government-enforced access controls, which may or may not involve medical prescriptions, an absence of commercialisation and advertising, and public-health policies designed to inform citizens of the risks associated with specific drugs and 'nudge' their conduct away from harmful behaviours. A partial analogy can be drawn with the approach of Western governments towards tobacco. Tobacco remains legal and the taxation from it constitutes a valuable source of government revenue. But increasing restrictions on smoking in public places, constraints on advertising and sponsorship, and prominent health warnings about the dangers of smoking, together with aggressive health policies to help smokers quit, have all conspired to make this practice far less socially acceptable than in the past. Another example is the epidemic of gin drinking which occurred in eighteenth-century Britain, the consequences of which were depicted by the artist William Hogarth in works such as *Gin Lane* and *The Rake's Progress*. In due course the worst effects of this epidemic were overcome by a regulation regime – the 1736 Gin Act, the 1750 Sale of Spirits Act and the 1751 Gin Act – which brought all sales under a strict lincensing system, increased tax and hiked fees for licencees.[11]

Advocates of legalisation and regulation accept that this approach will not of itself resolve all the problems associated with the misuse of drugs, nor is it intended to do so. The aim is quite simply to address the security issues that arise from a prohibition-based approach. Any regime which replaced prohibition would need to be adequately resourced and vigorously policed against the risks of illicit diversion from state-controlled supplies, smuggling and counterfeiting (according to the World Health Organisation, some 10% of the world's medicines are counterfeit, rising to 30% in the developing world, with anti-malaria medicines a particular favourite of counterfeiters.[12]) One of the criticisms made of a legalisation–regulation regime has been that while the countries of the developed world might have the capacity and resources to implement it effectively,

the same would not be true of developing countries. This is
the basis for former UNODC Executive Director Antonio
Maria Costa's contention that legalisation would give rise to
a major epidemic of addiction, with the burden falling disproportionately on countries in the developing world which lack
the resources to deal with the public-health and social consequences.[13] That it would present such countries with a new set
of challenges is not in doubt. The question is whether those
challenges could be met more effectively, at costs at least not
significantly higher than those incurred by current approaches
and with less collateral damage.

Determining the costs and benefits of introducing a legalisation and regulation regime is extremely difficult. The only
numbers we have are those associated with the prohibition
regime; we do not have comparable figures for the cost of a
legalisation and regulation regime, nor a clear idea of the
extent to which the costs of the former could be transferred
to the latter. A 2010 study by Jeffrey A. Miron and Katherine
Waldock of the Cato Institute attempts to estimate what such a
shift might mean for the US, based on the costs associated with
the status quo. The study estimates that a policy of total drugs
legalisation would save the US government $41.3 billion per
year (this being an estimate of the sum expended on prohibition enforcement), and that a further $46.7bn in revenue could
be raised through taxing drugs.[14] In principle, much if not all of
that revenue could be made available for treatment and public
education. These figures are based on assumptions, not least
the supposition that it might be feasible to permit all drugs
to be equally accessible and subject to taxes on consumption.
As such, they can at best only be regarded as illustrative. But
even these very rough calculations suggest that moving from
prohibition to legalisation and regulation might not impose
significant additional resource burdens on consumer coun-

tries – though allowance would have to be for the inevitable costs associated with any major policy shift, which experience suggests are generally much higher than anticipated – and could conceivably prove cost-neutral or better.

Applying such calculations to weak and fragile states is much harder, due to the very different conditions which apply in each. It is possible to argue that many of the resources currently devoted to security-led supply-control policies, whether indigenous or in the form of foreign assistance, could be diverted to public-health and economic-development programmes as the government of Colombia aspires to do. But there is no such obvious trade-off to be made in the case of West African states, whose expenditure on supply-control, including that element provided by the international community, falls far short of making a difference to public-health programmes. If legalisation were to translate into increased levels of consumption – there is no certainty that it would – development aid budgets would come under significant pressure as rehabilitation schemes demanded increased funding. For such states the key benefit of a shift comes in terms of the scope that offers, over time, for improved governance once the corrosive effects of narco-criminality are diminished.

Gauging the effect on criminal and non-state groups of a transition from prohibition to legalisation and regulation is also far from straightforward. Drugs have been the commodity which more than any other has primed the pump for the massive rise in organised criminality witnessed since the end of the Cold War. And they still account for a significant proportion of the profits of organised criminal groups – possibly as much as 50% – even though many of these groups have diversified into other lucrative activities such as people-smuggling, counterfeiting and cyber crime. Thus, in principle, collapsing the black market in drugs ought to have a significant beneficial impact in terms of reducing levels of violence and criminality. The reality is inevitably more complex than this: the manner and speed of any transition would be determined by the specific circumstances prevailing in the countries concerned. Organisations such as the Taliban and FARC, for whom the drugs trade represents a means to achieving a political end, are unlikely to be deterred by the loss of a single revenue stream, however substantial. Criminal groups whose strategic advantage lies precisely in their adaptability and resilience can be expected to pursue alternative revenue streams in ways that might be as destabilising as the drugs trade undoubtedly has been. In the short term, the end of the illicit drugs trade may well cause significant social and economic dislocation, as peasant cultivators who have come to rely on coca leaf or opium poppy to sustain their livelihoods are denied this option. But all these short-terms costs have to be weighed against the potential long-term benefits of eliminating a trade which has had such demonstrably damaging consequences.

The environment is one area that could well benefit from a shift to a legalisation regime. One of the underappreciated consequences of the drugs trade as currently constituted is a significant level of environmental damage arising out of illicit production. This was highlighted in a 2011 official study indicating that, between 2002 and 2009, deforestation resulting from coca production destroyed 188,000ha of Colombian forest. The same study speculated that, given the deforestation rate, 804,000ha could have been destroyed in the 1981–2009 period.[15] In 2008 this argument was used by Colombia's then Vice-President Francisco Santos, who sought to attract international attention to the drugs problem by claiming that in Colombia 300,000ha of primary rainforest was lost to illicit coca plantations each year.[16] And the environmental damage from such plantations is not limited to deforestation. As US Drugs Czar John Waters has observed,

> 600 million litres of so-called precursor chemical are used annually in South America for cocaine production. To increase yields, coca growers use highly poisonous herbicides and pesticides, including paraquat. Processors also indiscriminately discard enormous amounts of gasoline, kerosene, sulphuric acid, ammonia, sodium bicarbonate, potassium carbonate, acetone, ether and lime onto the ground and into nearby waterways.[17]

The area of damaged ecosystem cited by Santos appears significantly at odds with that cited by UNODC, which in 2010 reported 62,000ha of coca plantation in Colombia versus 61,200ha in Peru.[18] But the general point made by Santos stands, even though coca is not the only source of de-forestation and environmental degradation within the Andean region. Santos found that his appeal to the consciences of affluent Western drugs users fell on deaf ears; the linkage between their personal behaviour and its wider consequences proved too intangible to have resonance. But nobody contested the reality of the damage being done.

The opposition to legalisation

In spite of the uncertainties, there is equally no certainty that legalisation would necessarily be worse than the status quo; in contrast, there are some grounds for supposing that over time a shift to such a regime could deliver real benefits as drugs ceased to be the quick, easy way for criminals and non-state groups to raise revenues. The fact that the governments of some countries most directly affected are arguing for a rethink of present policies, as evidenced by a joint declaration by Latin American presidents and ministers at the XIII Tuxtla System for Dialogue in December 2011,[19] should of itself constitute an important incentive to stimulate thinking about ways in which evidence might be more effectively gathered to test how these alternatives might play out. It bears re-emphasising that the political and institutional obstacles to such a change remain formidable, with key political constituencies as yet unconvinced of the case for legalisation or any other option.

Especially for US politicians, who were historically the driving force behind the prohibition regime and continue to advocate hardline approaches, narcotics reform remains a 'third-rail' issue. As mentioned above, the Obama administration has sought to reconfigure domestic drugs policies in favour of a public-health approach. But when it comes to the international security dimension of counter-narcotics, the prevailing view in Washington is that current policies are working well; levels of cocaine consumption in the US are falling and the case of Colombia is seen as a model of how a campaign against narcotics trafficking and narco-terrorism can deliver effective results.[20] The US has been consistent in its criticism of states whose drugs policies are seen as deviating from a maximalist interpretation of the conventions: Switzerland in particular has come under attack for its policy of heroin maintenance dosages.

Nor is there greater appetite for a policy shift among other states with the power to instigate radical change. The People's Republic of China has been inoculated against a more liberal approach to counter-narcotics by its experience at the hands of the Western powers during the nineteenth and early twentieth centuries. This experience, characterised as the century of national humiliation – *bai nian guo chi* – has become the foundation myth and basis for continued legitimacy of the Chinese Communist Party, which believes that drugs represent an unmitigated evil. A similar approach is evidenced by the Russian Federation, which is now in the grip of a significant drugs epidemic with an estimated 3m heroin addicts and up to a million HIV/AIDS sufferers.[21] It is no exaggeration to say that the Russian state is in denial about the extent to which its own social and economic policies have created the circumstances for such high levels of drug use, preferring instead to talk of the need to reduce the supply of heroin emanating from Afghanistan. Neither in the Islamic world, nor in sub-Saharan Africa is there any obvious appetite for drugs-policy reform. And while Western states generally are moving from policies based on penalisation towards health-based demand management, few serving Western politicians have called publicly for a review of the prohibition regime.

Much of the political debate about drugs in those countries best placed to effect change focuses on domestic harms: the health problems of chronic users and the socially disruptive impact of low-level criminality. The security problems faced by producer and transit states, if they are considered at all, are generally viewed in terms specific to the particular locations rather than being seen in aggregate as a global security and development issue. An international narcotics-control system which has developed over the course of a century, with an almost exclusive focus on supply reduction, has given rise to some powerful communities with vested interests in the status quo. Achieving the diplomatic unanimity required to effect change is, it seems, an impossible task. Even comprehensive state failure in an entire region such as Central America might not suffice to persuade governments of the need for collective reconsideration.

Licit production

Having shouldered so many of the costs of enforcing prohibition, the developing world has failed to derive benefit from the other main declared purpose of the current international regime, which is to ensure adequate supplies of drugs for licit medical purposes, in particular pain relief and palliative care. In its 2004 annual report, the International Narcotics Control Board (INCB) observes that 'the low consumption of opioid analgesics for the treatment of moderate to severe pain, especially in developing countries, continues to be a matter of great concern … in 2003, six countries together accounted for 79% of global consumption of morphine … developing countries, while representing about 80% of the world's population, accounted for only 6%'. [22] Yet despite this, the INCB continues to maintain that the global supply of opiates is 'at levels well in excess of global demand'.

This can be explained by the reality that demand for opiates is determined not just by objective medical considerations, but also by a host of political and cultural factors. Many countries in the developing world are reluctant to countenance the widespread use of opiate-based medicines because of ill-founded fears of large-scale addiction or diversion, or simply because the health services in the countries concerned lack the capacity either to provide an estimate of demand or the mechanisms and resources to implement effective pain-management regimes. Even in countries where opiate-based medicines are widely used, there is considerable fluctuation in levels of use as between, for example, countries in the European Union. The INCB's argument, in effect, is that there is no point, and much risk, in accumulating substantial additional supplies unless and until better mechanisms can be devised both to estimate and meet potential global demand. For this reason, well-intentioned but ill-thought-out initiatives, such as the suggestion of buying Afghanistan's entire opium harvest for medical use, quite apart from the impracticalities of undertaking such an enterprise in what is still a war zone, have little relevance to the debate.[23]

Conclusion

International pressure for a rethink of the drugs prohibition regime is growing, particularly from Latin America, one of the regions of the developing world most seriously affected by drugs-related violence, instability and corruption. Serving politicians are now joining retired public figures in calling for current policies to be re-examined. Meanwhile, the prohibition regime has become entrenched due partly to institutional inertia and a stove-piped approach which limits the scope for challenging the status quo. But potential alternatives do exist and these cannot simply be dismissed as a leap into the dark. Even within the status quo, it is possible to envisage an application of the conventions which allows for greater diversity and experimentation, giving rise to more useful data on the basis of which existing policies might be reappraised.

A less restrictive approach to the applications of the conventions would not of itself address the security issues of most concern to the developing world. That would require the elimination of the global black market in drugs: a move from prohibition to a regime based on legalisation and regulation. The challenges this would entail cannot be underestimated. Even assuming that the political, cultural and ethical objections to such a change could be overcome, arrangements which have been put in place over the course of a century and become 'hard-wired' into international and national structures could not realistically be dismantled overnight. Nor is it possible to anticipate with full confidence what precisely would be the impact of collapsing the global black market in drugs on the security, stability and governance of those states and regions suffering most acutely from drugs-related destabilisation. Historical experience suggests that states take more time than anticipated to recover from serious internal conflicts, even if these do not assume the dimensions of full-blown civil wars. As Paul Collier has pointed out, 'the typical civil war lasts long enough, around seven years, but the damage persists well beyond the end of the conflict ... In many cases most of the costs of a civil war occur only once it is over.'[24] And there can be no certainty that funding saved on security-based supply-reduction programmes would easily translate into healthcare and economic development programmes of equivalent value. But all this said, there is enough evidence relating to legalisation and regulations regimes to indicate that a move in that direction would address many of the issues associated with the illicit drugs trade: the history of alcohol prohibition and the mechanics for regulating tobacco and licit pharmaceuticals offer useful insights into how such a regime might operate, though much more detailed work is needed, in particular looking at the costs of such a regime and considering how these might compare with the cost–benefit equation for prohibition.

CONCLUSION

An American tourist on a visit to his ancestral home in the south of Ireland became hopelessly lost in the narrow, winding, rural lanes. Eventually he came upon an elderly farmer from whom he sought directions. The farmer listened gravely, pondered for a while, then said, 'Well Sir, if I were you, I wouldn't start from here'. After 50 years, the Single Convention on Narcotic Drugs has failed to prevent the widespread production, trafficking and non-medical consumption of such drugs. Nor has it succeeded in ensuring that an adequate supply of such drugs is available for licit medical purposes other than in a few developed Western states, with the result that many patients suffering chronic or terminal illnesses receive inadequate or non-existent palliative care. Within consumer countries, long-term problem drug users have been socially marginalised and forced into a twilight world characterised by risky behaviours and significant harms, in particular the blood-borne transmission of HIV/AIDS through the sharing of needles. At the less serious end of the scale, many citizens have found themselves criminalised for being in possession of recreational doses of drugs, many of which are increasingly recognised by medical opinion as less harmful than licit substances like alcohol and less likely to give rise to the kind of anti-social behaviour widely associated with excessive consumption of the latter. In inner cities and other deprived areas of the developed world, entire communities have been blighted by the drugs economy and the associated high levels of violence, corruption and social breakdown. Within user countries, the bulk of counter-narcotics efforts have been focused on supply reduction – mainly interdictions and arrests. By comparison, few resources have been devoted to public education, health care and rehabilitation, though that is slowly starting to change.

Meanwhile, the problems of illicit drug consumption at a global level look set to get worse. Demand for strongly addictive drugs such as heroin and cocaine appears broadly to be levelling off in the developed world and in some cases, such as that of cocaine consumption in the United States, actually beginning to fall. But this is more than made up for by steadily rising usage elsewhere. Russia and Iran now have substantial populations of heroin addicts – in the latter case possibly as high as three million. And although there are few hard figures, there are indications that, within the newly emerging economies, levels of drug use are beginning to rise. In 2006, China had 1.14m registered drug users, half of whom injected intravenously; intravenous drug use accounted for 42% of the country's HIV/AIDS cases.[1] Given that in China drug users are compelled to undergo harsh detoxification regimes with no medical treatment or counselling, it is likely that the true total of China's drug users is much higher than 1.14m. In many ways the most worrying situation is to be found in some of the world's most impoverished countries, such as those in West Africa which have served as transit hubs for the cocaine and heroin trades and which entirely lack health care or social-welfare networks capable of dealing with growing levels of drug abuse.

It is on the developing world that the burden of combatting illicit drug production and trafficking has fallen to a disproportionate degree. The cases of Colombia and Afghanistan as producer states and Mexico, Central America and West Africa as transit regions are described in detail in earlier chapters. Of these only Colombia, a relatively prosperous state with functioning institutions and the benefit of political and practical support from the US, has succeeded in managing drugs-related violence down to the point where it no longer constitutes a national-security threat and can start to be addressed as a law and order problem. Even there, however, the gains registered are fragile and potentially reversible, and legacy issues of social and economic disruption are formidable. Cocaine production in Colombia may have decreased as a consequence of a better security environment, but neighbouring states such as Peru have more than made up the shortfall due to the balloon effect. In Mexico, the incidence of drugs-related violence began to level off in 2010, albeit at levels which by any standards would be considered alarmingly high. But violence has been displaced to the fragile states of Central America with even Costa Rica, long seen as a regional bastion of stability and prosperity, experiencing rising levels of drugs-related criminality.

In Afghanistan, the heroin trade helps fuel a long-running insurgency which is unlikely to end in 2014 with the draw-down of NATO/ISAF combat forces, whilst simultaneously perpetuating within the Afghan government levels of criminality and corruption which actively promote the conditions for the insurgency to flourish. The conflicting demands of the counter-insurgency and counter-narcotics agenda, with success in the former critically dependent upon securing the consent of a population for which opium production represents a social safety net, renders significant progress in the latter all but impossible. The consequence is manifested in growing levels

of heroin consumption and associated criminality in neighbouring states, including the former Soviet states of Central
Asia, which are inherently fragile and subject to high levels
of poverty. Some of West Africa's more fragile and economi-
cally underdeveloped states, though unlikely to succumb to
high levels of drugs-related violence, have been taken over and
comprehensively corrupted by narcotics-trafficking groups, to
the point where the latter secure the loyalty of local populations
by providing levels of social welfare far beyond the capacity of
states to match.

There is a growing consensus that the developing world has
been left to deal with problems that arise out of demand in the
developed world for substances which, because they are illegal,
acquire an inflated market value, with all the incentives this
provides for organised criminal groups. This was most clearly
articulated in the June 2011 report of the Global Commission on
Drugs Policy, set up by former presidents Fernando Cardoso,
Ernesto Zedillo and Cesar Gaviria. The key recommendation
of the report, that there needs to be a comprehensive rethink
of the global narcotics-control regime, has increasingly been
taken up by serving politicians in Latin America including Presidents Calderon of Mexico and Santos of Colombia,[2]
and is beginning to gather some international momentum.
Guatemalan President Otto Perez Molina has proposed the
legalisation of drugs in Central America to address high levels
of drugs-related violence there.[3]

But the obstacles to radical change cannot be underestimated. Many politicians – along with the representatives of
other constituencies involved in upholding the existing regime,
such as law-enforcement officers and international bureaucrats
– will privately express reservations about the efficacy of the
international drugs-control regime and argue for a rethink, but
will seldom express such thoughts publicly for fear of appear-

ing to be 'weak on drugs', with all the electoral liability that this entails. Within consumer countries, the social consequences of narcotics abuse seldom attract the attention of electorates other than on occasions when a particular drugs-related news story makes transitory headlines. Narcotics-fuelled destabilisation in the developing world tends to be seen as specific to the countries affected by it, rather than as a feature of a more generic complex of security, governance, human-rights, environmental and economic-development issues. There was scant mention, for example, of the wider drugs trade in international reports of deadly rioting that broke out in Monterrey Prison in northern Mexico on 20 February 2012. Western media outlets described the fighting, which led to 44 deaths and an undisclosed number of escapes, as gang rivalry between inmates from the Zetas and Gulf cartels, which may have been started deliberately as a diversion to allow some members to escape.[4] The phenomenon of transnational organised crime occupies an intermediate position in the minds of policymakers, who seem unsure at what point this ceases to be just a nuisance – an unavoidable tax on globalisation – and becomes a strategic threat in its own right. At an international level, the problem of narcotics has not attracted sustained focus from those policymakers with the power to effect change. There are in any case powerful constituencies opposed to such change, motivated either by considerations of morality – a factor whose importance cannot be underestimated – or by self-interest. As matters stand, the international regime for controlling narcotics refuses to countenance any alternative to a prohibition-based approach, on the basis of a counterfactual argument that the harms done by drugs would be considerably worse without the arrangements that have been put in place. Whether by accident or by design, the three conventions underpinning this regime have been subject to a restrictive, one-size-fits-all interpretation, which takes no account of the specific circumstances of particular countries and which bands together drugs with very different properties. Though the need to address demand issues is recognised, the reality is that the overwhelming focus of international drugs-control activities has been on supply-reduction policies, which take a heavy toll on the fragile and failing states whose circumstances are most propitious for the illicit cultivation of opium poppy and coca leaf.

It is relatively easy to assess the costs of existing counter-narcotics policies, though caution is needed in attributing to counter-narcotics policies the totality of security-related costs in fragile and failing states inherently vulnerable to such insecurity. Assessing what alternative policies might cost is far more difficult and is most easily done in relation to the consumer countries, where such experimentation as the conventions allow – or at the margins of what they allow – can offer some indication of the relative benefits of law-enforcement and public-health approaches. But the likely costs of a legalisation regime, whatever form that might take, are much harder to assess. The costs of establishing and policing such a regime – for it would need to be policed – and the degree to which legalisation might lead to a spike in global consumption, are issues where a great deal more detailed work is needed together with an international climate that encourages debate on such issues, rather than one that seeks to close such debate down. Meanwhile, caution is needed on the part of advocates of such an approach, particularly in terms of claims about the extent to which criminality and global instability might be reduced by a legalisation regime. Removing from the equation one of the most profitable and most easily trafficked sources of revenue for criminal groups is likely to have a beneficial impact over time, but this should not be equated with eliminating criminality or the threat posed by other non-state groups who currently derive significant revenues from the drugs trade.

In the absence of an international move to legalisation, there are measures that can be taken to mitigate the worst effects of current policies without overturning the existing order. The trend in consumer states to move away from criminalisation towards public health and rehabilitation can be continued and intensified, even if this challenges maximalist interpretations of how the conventions should be applied. Within such countries, law-enforcement efforts should increasingly move away from low-level interdictions and arrests towards a more strategic, intelligence-led approach, which focuses on the top-tier criminals who derive most benefit from the trade. The aim should be to target the proceeds of organised criminal groups. Consumer countries can also do more to provide practical assistance to states afflicted by drugs-related violence in areas such as capacity-building in the wider security sector; not just to the security forces but also judiciaries and civil-society groups. Addressing the human-rights dimension of such assistance presents some difficult dilemmas, which may discourage direct engagement. But such engagement can generate pressure in the direction of more enlightened policies and less reliance on the blunt instrument of military forces not trained or equipped to deal with the challenges posed by drugs-enabled non-state groups. Sensitivity is also required to ensure that states who accept such assistance retain their sense of sovereignty. In the best cases, some degree of shared sovereignty, with clearly agreed guidelines, may be the best approach. As in consumer countries, the focus of security and law enforcement needs to be on those at the top of the supply chain rather than on peasant cultivators simply trying to make a living. The economic benefits of this approach have been convincingly demonstrated.

Finally, drugs need to be taken out of their stovepipe and addressed as part of a holistic approach to security and development. Security and development are two constituencies which do not naturally see eye to eye. But the experience of humanitarian interventions since the war in Yugoslavia has provided examples which demonstrate the benefits of greater collaboration and integration of effort by these different communities in pursuit of common goals. International development agencies such as the United Kingdom's Department for International Development have recognised good security as a prerequisite for development and have resourced this sector accordingly. More consciously adopting counter-narcotics as part of a wider development agenda offers perhaps the best framework within which the status quo and alternatives to it can be scientifically debated.

1961 Single Convention on Narcotic Substances

Key points:

- Categorises all narcotic drugs into four schedules based on chemical makeup, pharmacology, and degree of restriction required;
- amalgamates nine pre-existing drug treaties into a single act;
- specifies special measures to be taken against opium poppy, poppy straw and cannabis; and
- recognises the relevance of socio-economic factors in determining drug use.

Principal aims:

- Restrict the cultivation, production, manufacture, trafficking and use of narcotic drugs to medical and scientific purposes;
- ensure the prevention of social and economic danger to

mankind as a result of the serious *evil* for the individual through addiction to narcotic drugs;

- enhance cooperation between states, NGOs, UN bodies and other relevant actors to better fight and prevent drug abuse; and
- present a unified front on international drug policy, incorporating states from all concerned regions.

Principal actors:
- Commission on Narcotic Drugs (CND)
- International Narcotics Control Board ('the Board')
- World Health Organisation (WHO)
- Economic and Social Council of the United Nations ('the Council')

Entry into Force: 13 December 1964
Signatories: 140

Summary of articles
Medical/scientific purposes (med/sci):
The 1961 Convention recognises the medical benefits of narcotics such as cannabis and opium derivatives and imposes a positive duty on the pertinent authorities to ensure that provision of medical narcotics is available to all. However, countries retain the right to implement total prohibition of cultivation and for this reason cohesion on the permissibility of cultivation for medical purposes appears difficult to achieve.

Multilateral data collection:
States are required to fulfil any information requests given by the Board, including but not limited to:
- Annual reports on achievement/failure of the convention's goals;

- updates on any legal developments related to aforementioned goals;
- statistics on illicit production, manufacture, and consumption of drugs;
- reports on any drug seizures, detailing measures taken to destroy contraband;
- quantity of drugs currently held within the country;
- amount of Drug-Arable land;
- methodology: Board responsible for validating the integrity of national data; and
- compliance: dissatisfaction with a signatory's efforts to achieve Convention goals will result in Board action.

Controls and regulations
Illicit trade and distribution:
Suggests the creation of a national agency exclusively for anti-trafficking efforts and promotes the increased collaboration of countries to halt drug traffic.

Licit trade and distribution:
Agents authorised by governments to engage in licit trade must have permits and are charged with providing accurate reports on activities and soliciting the appropriate certificates for exports and imports. Under a special provision, poppy straw import/export must be reported on quarterly basis. The amount of poppy straw must not exceed the demand estimates given to the Board in the previous annual report which is meant to prevent excess stockpiling.

Licit manufacturing:
Manufacturers must obtain periodical permits specifying the amounts of drugs they are entitled to manufacture in order to be properly licensed, but not for preparations. Stockpiling is to

be avoided at all costs; only the amount requisite for normal business will be permitted.

Licit cultivation:

Parties wishing to cultivate opium poppy for opium derivatives are required to set up a monopsonic system (a market system in which there is one buyer). The party must submit said system to all the controls of the licit trade and distribution and provide detailed information about the use of poppy straw for med/sci purposes. Import, export and production of Coca leaves are allowed only if the coca leaf is being used as a flavouring agent. Cannabis is subject to the same regulations as opium poppy, unless it is to be used for industrial purposes.

Penal provision
Possession:

Allowed only through medical prescriptions.

Extradition:

If an extradition treaty exists between the concerned parties then drug offences should qualify as extraditable; if not, then the convention offers itself as a legal base from which to conduct extradition. Parties reserve the right to refuse. As is often the case with drug trade, in the instance that the offense occurs in various territories, jurisdiction is given to the country that secures the offender.

Punishment:

The only punishment specified is imprisonment and 'other forms of liberty deprivation', but no specifics are given.

Preventing abuse:
'Four Es' of prevention:
1. early identification;
2. education;
3. edifying rehabilitation; and
4. emphatic reintegration.

Prevention will be achieved through the training of expert staff who will execute the aforementioned measures. Reference is made to public information campaigns and the creation of regional centres, but again no guide is given as to how to finance and provide these services.

Extra provisions

Any party may supplement the 1961 Convention with more severe measures. The convention places no limitation, scope, or contingencies on these extra mechanisms. Disputes between two parties will be mediated through mutual consultation and, should that fail, the International Court of Justice will intervene.

Schedules

- Schedule I: Cannabis and all its by-products, coca leaf, poppy straw, heroin, morphine, opium
- Schedule II: Codeine, nicocodeine, ethylmorphine (less strictly regulated)
- Schedule III: Preparations of substances filed under Schedules I and II
- Schedule IV: Cannabis and all its by-products, heroin, morphine (especially dangerous)

1971 UN Convention on Psychotropic Substances

Key points:

- Incorporates barbiturates, tranquilizers and amphetamines into the fight against drug use and trade, most notably: LSD, psilocybin, mescaline and THC;
- promotes multilateral research on medical substitute for amphetamines as they are deemed too dangerous for frequent use;
- 115 pyschotropic substances are regulated under the convention.

Principal aims:

Psychotropic substances fall outside the purview of the 1961 Convention, prompting the drafting of the 1971 Convention by the Commission of Narcotic Drugs to regulate those substances not covered by the 1961 Single Act Convention. The 1961 Scheduling excluded all substances that did not have similar effects to cocaine, heroin or cannabis.

The 1971 Convention departs from the Single Act by emphasising humanitarian concerns, such as the 'health of mankind', and calls for participants' renewed resolve to prevent and fight abuse. Continuation of the rigorous measures of 1961 would ensure that med/sci use is not hindered.

Entry into force: 16 August 1976

Signatories: 175

Summary of articles

The 1971 Convention offers states the option of deploying more rigorous control measures than those prescribed in the 1961 Convention.

Medical/scientific opium use
Restates the 1961 Convention's recognition of the medicinal utility of psychotropic substances.

Cannabis
A distinction is made between the cannabis plant and its active ingredient, tetrahydrocannabinol (THC).

Control and regulations of 1961 Convention
Reiterated the importance of identifying the medicinal, scientific and industrial usages of narcotic drugs and psychotropic substances, because novel methods of abuse or synthesis of new substances posed an obstacle to the conventions' aims. Reaffirmed support for process of introducing new drugs into schedules, which requires WHO and Commission recommendation.[1]

Traditional psychedelics
The convention follows its predecessor, restating the admissibility of psychotropic substances if they are deemed to be culturally relevant to indigenous persons this time in references to peyote, psilocybin and other hallucinogenics used in spiritual/religious ceremonies.

Treatment and prevention
There is more emphasis on substituting incarceration with other methods such as rehabilitation and also suggestions are made to fund public information campaigns and educate the public about substance abuse.

Penal provisions
As in the 1961 Convention, these are to be expressed within the confines of national constitutions and again, imprisonment is cited as the primary penal measure.

Classing drug offences as extraditable is strongly recommended, but not mandatory and indeed many countries object to these clauses in the 1961, 1971 and 1988 Conventions.

1988 UN Convention on Illicit Trafficking of Narcotic Drugs and Psychotropic Substances

Key points:

- Provides more adequate legal enforcement of the 1961 Convention to combat the organised-crime element of drug trafficking (a 1961 measure deemed insufficient by the parties to the convention due to ubiquitous rises in drug use and trade);
- makes explicit the nexus between human-rights violations and drug production and trafficking;
- focuses on the pejorative effect of the drug trade on socio-economic stability and security and highlights the pragmatic and ethical inadequacy of supply-side centred policies.

Principal aims:

The convention builds on the provisions laid out by the 1961 and 1971 Conventions, with variations on emphasis and a general shift of concerns to include: demand-side issues, user penalisation, user rehabilitation, organised crime, financing of drug trade, the reconciliation of national legal measures, and the conceptualisation of the war on drugs as also being the domain of developmental efforts and agencies (introducing the notion that political and economic security and human security are at stake.) It expands the scope of pro-active measures to include investigations into money laundering, smuggling tactics, more forceful eradication of cultivations.

Entry into force: 11 November 1990
Signatories: 170

Summary of articles

States and relevant agencies must work in unison to trace confiscated materials in order to accurately establish their origin. Like its predecessors, the convention criminalises possession of illicit substances. At the time of the signing of the accession, signatories openly expressed their doubts about the utility of prohibiting possession for personal use.

Like the two conventions preceding it (1961, 1971), the 1988 convention claims that consideration will be given to substances that have demonstrable 'traditional use' (article 14). The lack of consesnus over this article threatens the conventions' overarching principles of multilateralism and cooperation.

Eradicate illicit cultivation

Special consideration is given to the environmental effects of counter-narcotics tactics, particularly to the ecological damage that ensues from aggressive crop eradication.

Enable confiscation

Customary bank secrecy must be relaxed and all financial records related to drug trafficking distributed to all actors under the convention's mandates.

Extradition

The convention offers itself as a legal basis from which to conduct extraditions where no extradition treaty exists. Many parties to the convention directly rejected this provision in their reservations and remain open only to bilateral agreements.

Implications

The ambiguous language employed by the 1961, 1971 and 1988 conventions, especially that used to express legal obligations, attempts to respect national sovereignty whilst achieving the convention's aims so as to concert individual anti-drug efforts into a united front. However, the result is often that of discord, disunity and incoherence at the time of implementation, because the overwhelming majority of parties will not alter or compromise their existing legal and constitutional imperatives to accommodate the 1961, 1971 or 1988 Conventions.

* * *

For full official documents on the UN Conventions please follow these links:

1961: http://www.unodc.org/pdf/convention_1961_en.pdf
1971: http://www.unodc.org/pdf/convention_1971_en.pdf
1988: http://www.unodc.org/pdf/convention_1988_en.pdf

NOTES

Introduction

1   These are: The Single Convention on Narcotic Drugs 1961, the Convention on Psychotropic Substances 1971 and the United Nations Convention Against Illicit Traffic in Narcotic Drugs and Psychotropic Substances 1988. See Appendix I for more details.

2   UNODC, *World Drug Report 2010*, (Vienna: UNODC, 2010), p. 37.

3   Sarah Boseley, 'Alcohol More Harmful than Heroin or Crack', *Guardian*, 1 November 2010.

4   UNODC, *World Drug Report 2010*, p. 194.

5   David Nutt, 'Estimating Drug Harms: a Risky Business?', Eve Saville Memorial Lecture, London, 2009, p. 4. Available at http://www.crimeandjustice.org.uk/estimatingdrugharms.html.

6   DEA, *DEA Drug Information*, United States Drug Enforcement Administration, December 2011, http://www.justice.gov/dea/pubs/abuse/index.htm.

7   Daniel Mejia and Daniel M. Rico, 'La Microeconomia de la Produccion y Trafico de Cocaina en Colombia', *Documentos CEDE*, no. 19, 1 July 2010.

8   *Ibid.*, p. 18.

9   Discussion with author, 25 November 2010.

10 UNODC, *World Drug Report 2010*, pp. 31–3, 43, 65.

11 *Ibid.*, pp. 40, 71.

12 'Making Drug Control "Fit for Purpose": Building on the UNGASS Decade', *Report by the Executive Director of the United Nations Office on Drugs and Crime as a Contribution to the Review of the Twentieth Special Session of the General Assembly* (Vienna: Commission on Narcotic Drugs, March 2008), p. 10, http://www.idpc.net/sites/default/files/library/DrugControl_FFP_Bldg_UNGASSdecade.pdf.

13 UNODC, World Drugs Campaign, http://www.unodc.org/drugs/en/security-and-justice/index.html.

14 Peter Reuter and Franz Trautmann (eds), *Report on Global Illicit Drug Markets 1998–2007* (Brussels: European Commission, 2009), p. 23.

Chapter One

1 Frederick Allen, *Secret Formula* (New York: Harper Collins, 1994), pp. 35–6.

2 William B. McAllister, *Drug Diplomacy in the Twentieth Century* (London and New York: Routledge, 2000), p. 12.

3 Paul Gootenberg (ed), *Cocaine: Global Histories* (London: Routledge, 1999), p. 149.

4 *Ibid.*, pp. 14–6.

5 The heroin in question was diverted from licit Turkish production for medical purposes.

6 Alfred W. McCoy, *The Politics of Heroin in Southeast Asia* (New York: Harper Torchbooks, 1972).

7 Misha Glenny, *McMafia: Seriously Organised Crime* (London: Vintage, 2009), pp. 5–6.

8 Phil Williams, 'Transnational Organised Networks', http://www.rand.org/content/dam/rand/pubs/monograph_reports/MR1382/MR1382.ch3.pdf, p. 69.

9 Roberto Escobar, *The Accountant's Story: Inside the Violent World of the Medellín Cartel* (New York: Grand Central Publishing, 2010).

10 UNODC, 'Money-Laundering and Globalization', http://www.unodc.org/unodc/en/money-laundering/globalization.html.

11 Financial Action Task Force (FATF) http://www.fatf-gafi.org/document/57/0,3746,en_32250 379_322 35720_34432121_1_1_1_1,00.html.

12 Phil Williams, 'Transnational Criminal Organisations and International Security', *Survival*, vol. 36, no. 1, spring 1994, p. 96.

13 John Kerry, *The New War: The Web of Crime that Threatens America's Security* (New York: Simon and Schuster, 1997).

14 The total value of transnational organised crime is unknown but has been assessed by UNODC as between US$120 billion and US$360bn.

15 Barry Buzan, 'Security, the State, the "New World Order", and Beyond', in Ronnie D. Lipschutz (ed.), *On Security* (New York: Columbia University Press, 1995), pp. 205–9.

16 UNDP, *Human Development Report 1994* (New York and Oxford: Oxford University Press for UNDP, 1994).

17 Peter A. Lupsha, 'Transnational Organised Crime versus the Nation State', *Transnational Organised Crime*, vol. 2, no. 1, spring 1996, pp. 21–48.

18 Mats Berdal and Monica Serrano (eds), *Transnational Organised Crime and International Security: Business as Usual?* (London: Lynne Rienner Publishers, 2002), p. 15.

19 The World Bank, *World Development Report 2011* (Washington DC: The World Bank, 2011), p. 2.

20 Paul Collier and Anke Hoeffle, 'On Economic Causes of Civil War', Oxford Economic Papers no. 50, 1998, pp. 563–73; 'Greed and Grievance in Civil War', World Bank Policy Research Working Paper, no. 2,355, May 2000.

21 James D. Fearon, 'Why Do Some Civil Wars Last So Much Longer than Others?', *Journal of Peace Research*, vol. 41, no. 3, May 2010, pp. 283–4.

22 Jo Becker, 'Tiger at the Door', *Guardian*, 16 March 2006.

23 James Cockayne and Daniel Pfister, 'Peace Operations and Organised Crime', *GCSP Geneva Papers* 2, 2008, p. 14.

24 Michael L. Ross, 'Oil, Drugs and Diamonds: the Varying Role of Natural Resources in Civil War', in Karen

Ballentine and Jake Sherman (eds), *The Political Economy of Armed Conflict, Beyond Greed and Grievance* (London: Lynne Rienner Publishers, 2003), pp. 47–70.

25 Fernando Henrique Cardoso, Cesar Gaviria and Ernesto Zedillo, 'The War on Drugs is a Failure', *Wall Street Journal*, 23 February 2009.

Chapter Two

1 Julia Buxton, 'The Historical Foundations of the Narcotic Drug Control Regime', in Philip Keefer and Norman Loayza (eds), *Innocent Bystanders* (London: Palgrave MacMillan and the World Bank, 2010), p. 67.

2 William B. McAllister, *Drug Diplomacy in the Twentieth Century* (London, Routledge: 2000), p. 16.

3 *New York Times*, 8 February 1914, cited in The Lectric Law Library, *A History of Drug Use and Prohibition*, http://www.lectlaw.com/files/drg09.htm; *San Francisco Examiner*, 'Hugs' Dope Den Found, New Orgy Feared Drug-Crazed Gunmen, Car Traced To S.F. Underworld', *San Francisco Examiner*, 14 October 1926, reproduced by Schaffer Library of Drug Policy http://www.druglibrary.org/mags/examiner26.htm.

4 'Filipinos Stop Opium', *Washington Post*, 10 March 1906.

5 McAllister, *Drug Diplomacy in the Twentieth Century* p. 33.

6 The concept of gateway drugs continues to enjoy currency. But while there can be no doubting that some addicts have graduated from softer to harder substances, no clear causal connection has been established and it may be that addicts who have gone down this route are those who in any case have a greater genetic propensity to addiction. UNODC data collected over the long term show relatively consistent proportions between the global number of cannabis consumers and those consuming drugs such as heroin and cocaine, with little sign of large-scale migration from one category to the other. UNODC, *World Drug Report 2010*, pp. 152, 174, 195.

7 Mike Gray, *Drug Crazy: How We Got into this Mess and How We Can Get Out* (London: Random House, 1998).

8 Buxton, 'The Historical Foundations of the Narcotic Drug Control Regime', p. 79. Anslinger (and other US officials) thought that Europe did not have a strong enough approach to drug control, hence the US stayed out of the most important founding conventions (1928, 1936). Acting independently of the league meant that the US could implement its stricter approach and, given that other countries were very keen on cooperating with the US, the Americans were able to impose their own rules, even though such rules were against the spirit of cooperation at the core of the league.

9 Report of the (Canadian) Senate Special Committee on Illegal Drugs, vol. III, part IV and Conclusions, September 2002, p. 23, http://www.parl.gc.ca/Content/SEN/Committee/371/ille/rep/repfinalvol13-e.htm.

10 The relevant passage of Article 3 paragraph 2 of the convention reads:

'Subject to its constitutional principles and the basic concepts of its legal systems, each Party shall adopt such measures as may be necessary to establish as a criminal offence under its domestic law, when committed intentionally, the possession. Purchase or cultivation of narcotic drugs or psychotropic substances for personal consumption contrary to the provisions of the 1961 Convention, the 1961 Convention as amended or the 1971 Convention.' United Nations, *United Nations Convention against Illicit Traffic in Narcotic Drugs and Psychotropic Substances, 1988*, p. 13 http://www.unodc.org/unodc/en/treaties/illicit-trafficking.html.

11 Cindy Fazey, 'The UN, Drug Policies and the Prospects for Change', April 2003, http://www.fuoriluogo.it/arretrati/2003/apr_17_en.htm.

12 International Narcotics Control Board report for 2011, http://www.incb.org/pdf/annual-report/2010/en/AR 2010 English.pdf.

13 Alfred W. McCoy, 'Opium', http://opioids.com/opium/history/index.html.

14 Richard Nixon, 'Special Message to the Congress on Drug Abuse Prevention and Control', 17 June 1971, http://www.presidency.ucsb.edu/ws/?pid=3048#axzz1UoFCcK8K.

15 Richard Nixon, 'Message to the Congress Transmitting Reorganisation Plan 2 of 1973 Establishing the Drug Enforcement Agency', http://www.presidency.ucsb.edu/ws/index.php?pid=4159#axzz1UoFCcK8K.

16 McCoy, 'Opium'.

17 *Ibid*.

18 William Scobie, 'Reagan Declares War on "White Collar" Cocaine', *Observer*, 28 March 1982.

19 Martin Walker and Simon Tisdall, 'US Unveils Anti-drug Strategy', *Guardian*, 6 September 1989.

20 The concept of securitisation was developed by Barry Buzan, Ole Waever and Jaap de Wilde in *Security: A New Framework for Analysis* (Boulder, CO: Lynne Rienner Publishers, 1998). The essence of this concept is that an audience is persuaded that a particular situation constitutes an existential threat, which justifies extraordinary measures being taken to protect against it. The concept is state-centric and tends to result in the application of military solutions to non-military problems.

21 Daniel Mejia, 'Evaluating Plan Colombia' in Keefer and Loayza (eds), *Innocent Bystanders*, p. 40.

22 Alba Hesselroth, 'Struggles of Security in US Foreign Drug Policy towards Andean Countries', *Peace Studies*, no. 5, July 2004, p. 16.

23 US Department of Justice (Bureau of Justice Statistics), *Correctional Population in the United States, 2010*, December 2011, p. 1, http://www.bjs.gov/content/pub/pdf/cpus10.pdf.

24 Franklin E. Zimrin, 'How New York Beat Crime', *Scientific American*, August 2011.

25 'Rough Justice: Too Many Laws, Too Many Prisoners', *Economist*, 22 July 2010, http://www.economist.com/node/16636027.

26 Malaysia's mandatory death penalty applies to those found in possession of 15 grams of heroin or 200 grams of marijuana.

27 Seventeen countries have either decriminalised or legalised the possession of some drugs for personal use. These are: Argentina (marijuana), Australia (marijuana in some states), Belgium (marijuana),

Canada (marijuana for industrial and medical use), Czech Republic (all drugs), Estonia (marijuana), Finland (marijuana for medical use), Israel (marijuana for medical use), Mexico (all drugs), the Netherlands (marijuana), Paraguay (marijuana, cocaine and heroin), Peru (marijuana), Portugal (all drugs), Spain (marijuana), Switzerland (supervised injection of heroin), the United States (marijuana in some states) and Uruguay (possession of drugs for personal use was never criminalised). In addition, possession of marijuana has effectively been decriminalised in Brazil, Cambodia, Costa Rica, Pakistan and Venezuela.

[28] Reuter and Trautmann, 'A Report on Global Illicit Drug Markets 1998–2007', Rand Corporation and Trimbos Institute for the European Commission, 2010, p. 16, http://ec.europa.eu/justice/anti-drugs/files/report-drug-markets-short_en.pdf.

[29] UNODC, *World Drug Report 2008*, p. 216, http://www.unodc.org/documents/WDR_2008/WDR_2008_eng_web.pdf.

Chapter Three

[1] Tom Feiling, *The Candy Machine: How Cocaine Took Over the World* (London: Penguin Books, 2009), p. 29.

[2] Vanda Felbab-Brown, *Shooting Up: Counterinsurgency and the War on Drugs* (Washington DC: Brookings Institution Press, 2010) pp. 71–2.

[3] Crack cocaine is simply powdered cocaine mixed with baking soda and water and baked into a rock. When heated, the rock releases a vapour, giving a 'high' which is both instantaneous and far more intense than that experienced by the more conventional method of 'snorting' powdered cocaine. Unlike snorting, the effect of which is conditioned by the limited absorptive capacity of the nasal tissues, there is no limit to the number of successive highs that can be experienced with crack.

[4] Feiling, *The Candy Machine*, p. 54.

[5] Rensselaer W. Lee, 'Perverse Effects of Andean Counternarcotics Policy', *Orbis*, vol. 46, no. 3, summer 2002, pp. 537–54, http://www.fpri.org/orbis/4603/lee.perverseeffectsandeancounternarcotics.pdf.

[6] Roberto Escobar and David Fisher, *The Accountant's Story* (New York and Boston, MA: Grand Central Publishing, 2009).

[7] For a detailed account of the life and death of Pablo Escobar, see Mark Bowden, *Killing Pablo: The Hunt for the Richest, Most Powerful Criminal in History* (London: Atlantic Books, 2001).

[8] Feiling, *The Candy Machine*, p. 169.

[9] Norman A. Bailey, 'La Violencia in Colombia', *Journal of Inter-American Studies*, vol. 9, no. 4, October 1967, pp. 561–75.

[10] For an account of FARC's strategic evolution based on captured FARC documentation, see IISS, IISS Strategic Dossier, *The FARC Files: Venezuela, Ecuador and the Secret Archive of 'Raul Reyes'* (London, IISS: 2011).

[11] Lee, 'Perverse Effects of Andean Counternarcotics Policy', p. 541.

12 Daniel Rico, former counter-narcotics adviser to the Colombian Defence Ministry, speaking at The International Institute for Strategic Studies Global Strategic Review, Geneva, 12 September 2009.

13 Plan Colombia was established to run until 2006 and was later given a one-year extension. Plan Patriota started in 2004. There was some overlap between the two plans in terms of duration and source of funding. For instance, funding from some activities under Plan Patriota came from the budget for Plan Colombia. The more recent National Consolidation Plan (announced in 2007) was part of the same family of separate initiatives developed in Colombia over the past decade.

14 Andres Pastrana Arango, *La Palabra Bajo Fuego* (Bogotá: Planeta, 2005), pp. 48–51.

15 Colombia's other main insurgent group, the Ejercito de liberacion Nacional (ELN), maintained a moral and ideological aversion to the narcotics trade, possibly attributable to its origins in liberation theology. The ELN had no such moral scruples about involvement in extortion and kidnapping, which provided the bulk of its finances.

16 IISS, *The FARC Files*.

17 United States Government Accountability Office, 'Plan Colombia', *Report to the Honourable Joseph R. Biden, Jr., Chairman, Committee on Foreign Relations, U.S. Senate* (Washington DC: GAO, October 2008), p. 14, http://ccai-colombia.org/files/primarydocs/0810USGAO.pdf.

18 Ministero de Defensa de Colombia (Dirección de Estudios Sectoriales), *Logros de la Política Integral de Seguridad y Defensa para la Prosperidad – PISDP*, October 2011, http://www.mindefensa. gov.co/irj/go/km/docs/Mindefensa/ Documentos/descargas/estudios%20 sectoriales/info_estadistica/Logros_ Sector_Defensa.pdf.

19 *Ibid.*

20 IISS, *The FARC Files*.

21 IISS, 'The Downfall of Alfonso Cano', *IISS Strategic Comments*, vol. 17, no. 44, November 2011.

22 Statistics obtained by author in the course of meetings with a range of Colombian government agencies during November 2010.

23 General Oscar Naranjo, Head of the Colombian National Police to author, November 2010.

24 Human Rights Watch, *Paramilitaries' Heirs: The New Face of Violence in Colombia*, 3 February 2010, pp. 3–7, http:// www.hrw.org/en/reports/2010/02/03/ paramilitaries-heirs.

25 Ricardo Rocha Garcia, *Las Nuevas Dimensioned de Narcotrafico en Colombia*, (UNODC and Ministerio de Justicia y del Derecho de Colombia, 2011), p. 25, http://www.unodc.org/colombia/es/ index.html.

26 UNODC, *World Drug Report 2010*, pp. 161–2.

27 Dr Daniel Mejia of the University of the Andes has undertaken a study covering the period 2000–08, which suggests that claims of glyphosates being responsible for skin lesions are probably unfounded and that these lesions can equally be explained by the use of noxious chemicals such as sulphuric acid used to make coca base. No comparable study has yet taken place of other harms allegedly inflicted by glyphosates, such as respiratory difficulties, spontaneous abortions and spinal cord damage. Discussion with author, 22 November 2010.

28 Discussion with author in Bogotá, November 2010.

29 Presidency of the Republic – Ministry of Defence, *Democratic Security and Defence Policy*, 2003, http://usregsec. sdsu.edu/docs/Colombia2003.pdf; USAID, *USAID/OTI's Initial Governance Response Program In Colombia. A Final Evaluation*, April 2011, http:// csis.org/files/publication/110701_ Colombia_Evaluation.pdf; Jack Kimball, 'Colombia Vows to Break Up Drug Gangs, Beat Rebels', Reuters, 24 May 2011, http://www.reuters. com/article/2011/05/24/us-colombia-security-idUSTRE74N8IV20110524.

30 Salomon Kalmanowitz, University of the Andes, in discussion with author, 22 November 2010.

31 UNODC, *World Drug Report 2010*, p. 48.

32 UNODC, 'UNODC Reveals Devastating Impact of Afghan Opium. How the World's Deadliest Drug Feeds Addiction, Crime and Insurgency', 21 October 2009, http://www.unodc.org/ unodc/en/press/releases/2009/october/ unodc-reveals-devastating-impact-of-afghan-opium.html.

33 UNODC, *World Drug Report 2010*, p. 48.

34 David MacDonald, *Drugs in Afghanistan: Opium, Outlaws and Scorpion Tales* (London: Pluto Press, 2007), p. 61, citing UNODC.

35 UNODC, *World Drug Report 2010*, p. 138; UNODC, *World Drug Report 2011* (Vienna: UNODC, 2011), p. 58.

36 UNODC, 'Opium Production in Afghanistan Shows Increase; Prices Set to Rise', 11 October 2011, http://www. unodc.org/unodc/en/frontpage/2011/ October/opiumproductioninafghanistan showsincreasepricessettorise.html.

37 UNODC, *World Drug Report 2010*, p. 35.

38 *Ibid.*, p. 137.

39 The reasons for the Taliban decision to ban opium for one year remains the subject of debate. Part of the explanation might be that it was at that point seeking international recognition for the regime and saw this as one way to burnish its credentials. But it may also be the case that previous high levels of production had led to a glut and a corresponding drop in prices, and that the move was an attempt at market correction.

40 James Cockayne and Daniel Pfister, 'Peace Operations and Organised Crime', p. 17.

41 Barnett Rubin, *Road to Ruin: Afghanistan's Booming Opium Industry* (New York: Center on International Co-operation and Washington DC: Center for American Progress, 7 October 2004), http://www.gtz.de/de/ dokumente/en-road-ruin-opium-afg. pdf.

42 Thom Shanker, 'Pentagon Sees Anti-drug Effort in Afghanistan', *New York Times*, 25 March 2005.

43 Judy Dempsey, 'NATO Allows Strikes on Afghan Drug Sites. Ministers Sign to Major Strategic Shift', *International Herald Tribune*, 11 October 2008.

44 David MacDonald, *Drugs in Afghanistan*, p. 65.

45 Jerome Starkey, 'US Army to Wage War on Drugs by Wiping out Afghan Poppy Fields', *Mail Online*, 13 October 2008, http://www.dailymail.co.uk/ news/article-1077253/US-army-wage-war-drugs-wiping-Afghan-poppy-fields.html.

46 Ben Farmer, 'Britain to Continue Poppy Eradication in Afghanistan Despite US Reversal', *Telegraph*, 28 June 2009, http://www.telegraph.co.uk/ news/worldnews/asia/afghanistan/

5674309/Britain-to-continue-poppy-eradication-in-Afghanistan-despite-US-reversal.html. For a timeline of eradication-related violence see IISS, 'Afghanistan: Timeline 2008', *The Armed Conflict Database*, http://www.iiss.org/publications/armed-conflict-database/.

47 'NATO Rejects Russia's Demand to Destroy Afghan Poppy Fields', *Pravda*, 24 March 2004, http://engforum.pravda.ru/index.php?/topic/204363-nato-rejects-russias-demand-to-destroy-afghan-poppy-fields/.

48 Akhunzada claimed he had confiscated the drugs and had been planning to destroy them.

49 The fighting season in Afghanistan typically starts in April and continues through the autumn.

50 Stanley A. McChrystal, *Commander's Initial Assessment* (Kabul: ISAF Headquarters, 30 August 2009), http://media.washingtonpost.com/wp-srv/politics/documents/Assessment_Redacted_092109.pdf.

51 Sally McNamara, 'Training Afghanistan's Security Forces: NATO Has Made Solid Progress', *Web Memo* 3295, 16 June 2011, http://www.heritage.org/research/reports/2011/06/natos-solid-progress-in-training-afghanistans-security-forces.

52 Jayshree Bajaria, 'Security Transition in Afghanistan', *Analysis Brief*, 22 March 2011, http://www.cfr.org/afghanistan/security-transition-afghanistan/p24456.

53 CIA, 'Afghanistan', *The World Factbook* (last updated 14 July 2011), https://www.cia.gov/library/publications/the-world-factbook/geos/af.html.

54 McNamara, 'Training Afghanistan's Security Forces'. Heritage Foundation ,16 June 2011.

55 Jonathan Burch and Hamid Shalizi, 'Security Deteriorating in Afghanistan, Life "Untenable"– ICRC', Reuters, 15 March 2011.

56 Susanne Koebl, 'US Cuts Aid After Millions Siphoned Off to Dubai', *Der Spiegel*, 7 May 2010.

57 Jon Boone, 'The Financial Scandal that Broke Afghanistan's Kabul Bank', *Guardian*, 16 June 2011.

58 Discussion with author, January 2011.

59 Barak Obama, 'Full text of President Obama's Speech on Afghanistan', *The Cable*, 22 June 2011, http://thecable.foreignpolicy.com/posts/2011/06/22/full_text_of_president_obamas_speech_on_afghanistan.

60 Toby Dodge and Nicholas Redman (eds), *Afghanistan to 2015 and Beyond* (Abingdon: Routledge for IISS, 2011).

Chapter Four

1 Robert Bunker, 'Strategic Threat: Narcos and Narcotics Overview', *Small Wars & Insurgencies,* vol. 21, no. 1, 2010, p. 17.

2 Monica Serrano, 'Drug Trafficking and the State of Mexico', in Richard Friman (ed.), *Crime and the Global Political Economy* (Boulder, CO: Lynne Rienner Publishers, 2009), p. 145.

3 Serrano, 'Drug Trafficking and the State of Mexico', pp. 145–50.

4 Peter Reuter, 'Eternal Hope: America's Quest for Narcotics Control', *Public Interest,* vol. 79, spring 1985, p. 80.

Turkey later overturned the ban, but licensed its opium production for medical purposes.

5 UNODC, *The Globalization of Crime. A Transnational Organized Crime Threat Assessment* (Vienna: UNODC, 2010), p. 87.

6 'The New Federation Breaks with La Familia Michoacana and the Gulf Cartel / It's going after the Zetas', mexico.vg , 2 January 2011, http://www.mexico.vg/mexicos-drug-cartels/the-new-federation-is-going-after-the-zetas/1325.

7 Stratfor, 'Kaibiles: The New Lethal Force in the Mexican Drug Wars', *Stratfor*, 25 May 2006.

8 Peter Chalk, *The Latin American Drug Trade. Scope, Dimensions, Impact, and Response* (Santa Monica, CA: RAND, 2011), pp. 24–30; Tom Feiling, *The Candy Machine*, pp. 141–9.

9 IISS, 'Mexico (Cartels)', *The Armed Conflict Database*; BBC, 'Mexico Drug War Deaths over Five Years Now Total 47,515', BBC, 12 January 2012.

10 Bunker, 'Strategic Threat', pp. 13–5.

11 Chalk, *The Latin American Drug Trade*, pp. 41–3.

12 Bunker and Sullivan, 'Cartel Evolution Revisited', p. 32.

13 Eduardo Castillo, 'Refusal to Join Drug Gang Likely Led to Massacre of Mexican Migrants', Associated Press, 21 August 2010, http://www.cleveland.com/world/index.ssf/2010/08/refusal_to_join_drug_gang_like.html.

14 Daniel Sabet, 'Police Reform in Mexico: Advances and Persistent Obstacles', *Working Paper Series on U.S.–Mexico Security Collaboration*, May 2010, pp. 8–13, 18–21,

15 'Spiralling Drug Violence in Mexico', *IISS Strategic Comments*, vol. 14, no. 8, 2008.

16 IISS, *The Chart of Conflict 2009* (London: IISS, 2009).

17 'Turning to the Gringos for Help', *Economist*, 27 March 2010, p. 52.

18 Dianne Feinstein, Charles Schumer and Sheldon Whitehouse, *Halting U.S. Firearms Trafficking to Mexico. A Report by Senators Dianne Feinstein, Charles Schumer and Sheldon Whitehouse to the United States Senate Caucus on International Narcotics Control*, 112th Congress. first Session (Washington DC: June 2011), p. 2.

19 Nick Miroff and William Booth, 'Mexico's 2012 Vote is Vulnerable to Narco Threat', *Washington Post*, 16 January 2012, http://www.washingtonpost.com/world/americas/mexico-2012-vote-vulnerable-to-narco-threat/2011/12/21/gIQAny4i1P_story.html.

20 David Shirk, 'The Drug War in Mexico. Confronting a Shared Threat', *Council Special Report*, no. 60, March 2011, p. 9.

21 *Ibid.*, pp. 9–10.

22 Tim Reid, 'Hillary Clinton's "War Cabinet" Sweeps in to Mexico for Drugs Summit', *Times*, 24 March 2010.

23 Diana Negroponte, 'Pillar IV of "Beyond Merida": Addressing the Socio-Economic Causes of Drug Related Crime and Violence in Mexico', *Working Paper Series on U.S.–Mexico Security Cooperation*, 7 July 2011, pp. 4–5.

24 A number of corruption scandals have been brought to light involving government officials, the judiciary, the police, the army and even the Catholic Church. Officials have been accused of favouring certain cartels while encouraging the fight against others. Federal and city police officers have been charged with running drug trafficking rings. Judges are known for acquitting cartel members

despite undisputable evidence of their activities.

25 UNODC, *United Nations Convention against Corruption*, May 2011 http://www.unodc.org/unodc/en/treaties/CAC/signatories.html.

26 Transparency International, *Corruption Perception Index 2011*, http://cpi.transparency.org/cpi2011/results/.

27 Luz Nagle, 'Corruption of Politicians, Law Enforcement, and the Judiciary in Mexico and Complicity Across the Border', *Small Wars & Insurgencies*, vol. 21, no. 1, 2010, pp. 95–122.

28 Nagle, 'Corruption of Politicians', pp. 111–12.

29 Bunker and Sullivan, 'Cartel Evolution Revisited', pp. 34–5. Phase one cartels are those following the model of the Colombian Medellin cartel that positioned itself as a direct and aggressive competitor of the state trying to gain the upper hand both politically and militarily. This model involves a very hierarchical structure, tactically efficient but lacking a strategic outlook. The phase two cartels are best represented by the Cali cartel, also from Colombia. They act as subtle co-opters and use violence symbolically, rather than indiscriminately (as in the case of phase one) and rely on corruption extensively. They function through a cell-based network with the top leadership remaining anonymous.

30 Shirk, 'The Drug War in Mexico', p. 11.

31 Tyler Bridges, 'Coverage of Drug Trafficking and Organized Crime in Latin America and the Caribbean', in Guillermo Franco and Fabian Cardenas, *Coverage of drug trafficking and organized crime in Latin America and the Caribbean*, report from the 8th Austin Forum on Journalism in the Americas, Austin, 17–18 September 2010, p. 8.

32 'First Honduras Cocaine Laboratory Discovered', *BBC*, 10 March 2011.

33 IISS, *The 2009 Chart of Conflict*.

34 'The Tormented Isthmus', *Economist*, 14 April 2011; 'El Salvador Head Apologises for 1981 El Mozote Massacre', *BBC*, 17 January 2012, http://www.bbc.co.uk/news/world-latin-america-16589757.

35 US Department of State, Bureau of International Narcotics and Law Enforcement Affairs, *International Narcotics Control Strategy Report (INCSR)*, 3 March 2011, http://www.state.gov/p/inl/rls/nrcrpt/2011/index.htm.

36 The White House, Office of the Press Secretary, *Presidential Memorandum – Major Illicit Drug Transit or Major Illicit Drug Producing Countries*, 16 September 2010, http://www.whitehouse.gov/the-pressoffice/2010/09/16/presidential-memorandum-major-illicit-drug-transit-or-major-illicit-drug.

37 The World Bank, *World Development Report 2011* (Washington DC: The World Bank, 2011), p. 58.

38 Mitchell Koss, 'Central America's Bloody Drug Problem', *CNN*, 19 January 2012, http://edition.cnn.com/2012/01/19/world/americas/narco-wars-guatemala-honduras/.

39 Jose Ortega, 'San Pedro Sula (Honduras) la ciudad más violenta del mundo; Juárez, la segunda', *Seguridad, Justicia y Paz*, 11 January 2012 http://www.seguridadjusticiaypaz.org.mx/biblioteca/view.download/5/145. 'The Cost of a Coup', *Economist*, 9 June 2011.

40 The World Bank, *World Development Report 2011*, p. 4.

41 *Ibid.*, p. 57.

42 *Ibid.*

43 'The Tormented Isthmus'.

44 US Department of State, *2010 Human Rights Report: El Salvador*, 8 April

2011, http://www.state.gov/g/drl/rls/hrrpt/2010/wha/154505.htm.

45 US Department of State, *Honduras Country Specific Information*, http://travel.state.gov/travel/cis_pa_tw/cis/cis_1135.html.

46 Eddy Coronado, 'Llama ignorantes a quienes piden Estado de Sitio nacional', *Siglo21*, 26 May 2011, http://www.s21.com.gt/nacionales/2011/05/26/llama-ignorantes-quienes-piden-estado-sitio-nacional.

47 United States Senate Caucus on International Narcotics Control, *Responding to Violence in Central America*, 112th Congress, First Session, September 2011, p. 19.

48 International Crisis Group, 'Guatemala: Drug Trafficking and Violence', *Latin America Report* No. 39, 11 October 2011, pp. 3–4.

49 *Ibid.*, pp. 4–5.

50 United States Senate Caucus on International Narcotics Control, *Responding to Violence in Central America*, pp. 30–1.

51 Jeanna Cullinan, 'New Wave of Vigilanteism Hits Guatemala Tourist Spot', *InSight Crime*, 4 November 2011, http://insightcrime.org/insight-latest-news/item/1793-new-wave-of-vigilanteism-hits-guatemala-tourist-spot.

52 Stephen Ellis, 'West Africa's International Drug Trade', *African Affairs*, vol. 108, no. 431, 2009, pp. 173–80.

53 Ellis, 'West Africa's International Drug Trade', pp. 183–5.

54 UNODC, *World Drug Report 2006* (Vienna: UNODC, 2006), p. 17.

55 INCB, *Report of the International Narcotics Control Board for 2005*, E/INCB/2005/1 (New York: United Nations, 2006), p. 45.

56 UN, 'European Cocaine Market Continues to Rise, UN Anti-drugs Chief Warns', UN News Centre, 11 May 2011, http://www.un.org/apps/news/story.asp?NewsID=38333&Cr=illicit+drugs&Cr1.

57 UNODC, *World Drug Report 2011*, (Vienna: UNODC, 2011), p. 166. In a 2008 paper the UNODC Deputy representative for West and Central Africa outlined the division of labour for the trafficking of cocaine destined for Europe along three categories of actors. First are the foreign operators – mainly Latin Americans, but also Italians, Galicians and Lebanese – in charge of transporting multi-tonne shipments of narcotics from Latin America to West Africa. Second are African local groups – primarily Nigerians and Ghanaians – who are the heirs of 1980s–1990s African traffickers discussed earlier in this chapter. These criminals buy directly from the foreign operators and then re-sell cocaine regionally or in Europe. The third players in this market are the freelancers, i.e. Europeans or West Africans who smuggle very small quantities, up to two kilograms, into Europe, taking advantage of the fact that they have residency entitlement (Amado Philip de Andres, 'West Africa Under Attack: Drugs, Organised Crime and Terrorism as the New Threats to Global Security', *UNISCI Discussion Paper* 16, January 2008, pp. 210–11).

58 Kwesi Aning, interview with the authors, January 2011.

59 Europol, *EU Organised Crime Threat Assessment 2011* (The Hague: Europol, 28 April 2011), pp. 7–15. Cocaine arriving from Latin America in bulk shipments is usually stored, sometimes for several months, before being broken down in 100–200 kilogram parcels later moved northward using a

variety of means ranging from human mules to motorbikes and commercial cargoes. Sometimes drugs are stuffed inside African crafts or cosmetics. Once they reach Africa's northern coast, drugs are moved by boat to Galicia and then dispatched across Europe (International Liaison Unit spokesperson, interview with the author, January 2011). The routes used are often well established paths used to smuggle goods across the Sahel for centuries and where it is believed that groups affiliated with al Qaeda in the Islamic Maghreb may allow transit through the desert in exchange for money. More recently, West African traffickers have been exploiting countries in Eastern Europe, mainly Bulgaria, via Turkey and the Balkans, as entry point into the European market, taking advantage of less stringent controls in those countries. Often these routes included legs in Somalia, the Persian Gulf and Russia (Europol, *EU Organised Crime Threat Assessment 2011*, p. 10).

60 'West Africa Drugs Trafficking "Increasingly Sophisticated"', BBC, 21 June 2011.

61 Drew Hinshaw, 'West Africa's Cocaine Trade has Doubled in Five Years, UN Agency Estimates', Bloomberg, 25 May 2011.

62 Drew Hinshaw, 'West Africa Rising: Heroin, Cocaine Traffickers and More

Buyers at Home', *Christian Science Monitor,* 21 June 2011.

63 Remar Ghana staff, interview with the author, January 2011.

64 Vanda Felbab-Brown, 'The West African Drug Trade in Context of the Region's Illicit Economies and Poor Governance', Presentation to Conference on Drug Trafficking in West Africa, Arlington, VA, 14 October 2010. See also Tristan McConnell, 'President Joao Bernardo Vieira of Guinea-Bissau Assassinated by Army', *Times,* 3 March 2009; Jonathan Miller, 'Drug Barons Turn Bissau into Africa's First Narco-state', *Independent,* 18 July 2007.

65 'West Africa's Cocaine Coast', *IISS Strategic Comments,* vol. 17, no. 21, May 2011.

66 James Cockayne and Phil Williams, *The Invisible Tide: Towards an International Strategy to Deal with Drug Trafficking Through West Africa* (New York: International Peace Institute, 2009), pp. 12, 17.

67 'Dealers on a High', *Africa Confidential,* vol. 51, no. 11, 2010.

68 Jose Augusto Duarte, 'West Africa and the European Union: Key Areas and Possible Response Measures', *Portuguese Journal of International Affairs,* vol. 4, autumn/winter 2010, pp. 8–10.

69 The World Bank, *World Development Report 2011*, p. 218.

Chapter Five

1   Matthias Schwartz, 'A Massacre in Jamaica', *New Yorker*, 12 December 2011.

2   Randall C. Archibald, 'Trinidad and Tobago Declares Emergency Over Drug Crime', *New York Times*, 24 August 2011.

3   J. Githongo and N. Wainaina, 'Kenya: Drugs – the Final Frontier',17 December 2011, http://allafrica.com/stories/201112190255.html.

4   Ethan Nadelmann, 'Drug Prohibition in the United States: Costs, Consequences and Alternatives', *Science*, vol. 245, no. 4,921, 1 September 1989, pp. 939–47.

5   Caitlin Elizabeth Hughes and Alex Stevens, 'What Can We Learn From the Portuguese Decriminalisation of Illicit Drugs?', *British Journal of Criminology*, vol. 50, no. 6, November 2010, pp. 999–1,000.

6   C. Peter Rydell and Susan S. Everingham, *Controlling Cocaine: Supply Versus Demand Programmes*, (Santa Monica, CA: Rand Corporation, 1994).

7   US Office of National Drug Control Policy homepage, http://www.whitehouse.gov/ondcp.

8   Andrew Taylor, 'House Passes $1T Budget Bill, Avoids Shutdown', Associated Press, 16 December 2011, http://news.yahoo.com/house-passes-1t-budget-bill-avoids-shutdown-185348086.html.

9   Robin Room and Peter Reuter, 'How Well do International Drug Conventions Protect Public Health?', *Lancet*, vol. 379, no. 9,810, 7 January 2012, pp. 84–91.

10 "After the War on Drugs: Blueprint for Regulation", Transform Drug Policy Foundation, 2009, http://www.tdpf.org.uk/downloads/blueprint/Transform_Drugs_Blueprint.pdf.

11 The craze was fuelled by imports of cheap gin from the Netherlands, though distilleries in the UK quickly cottoned on to the popularity of the drink, while landowners grew rich from growing the grain needed to make it. The first attempt to curb the craze, the 1736 Gin Act, was so draconian that it drove the trade underground, eventually forcing the government to abandon some of its measures. Later measures introduced to tackle supply, particularly from disreputable merchants selling low-quality gin, included a ban on sales from distilleries to unlicensed merchants, and a requirement that licensed retailers should be substantial property holders.

12 WHO, General Information on counterfeit medicines, http://www.who.int/medicines/services/counterfeit/overview/en/index.html.

13 Antonio Maria Costa, 'Legalise Drugs and a Worldwide Epidemic of Addiction Will Follow', *Observer*, 5 September 2010.

14 Jeffrey A. Miron and Kathrine Waldock, 'The Budgetary Impact of Drug Prohibition', The Cato Institute, 27 September 2010.

15 Rocha, *Las Nuevas Dimensioned de Narcotrafico en Colombia*, pp. 130–1.

16 Sandra Laville, 'Cocaine Users are Destroying the Rainforest – at 4 Square Metres a Gram', *Guardian* 19 November 2008 http://www.guardian.co.uk/world/2008/nov/19/cocaine-rainforests-columbia-santos-calderon.

17 Walters, 'The Other Drug War'.

18 UNODC, *World Drug Report 2011*, p. 101.

19 XIII Cumbre de Jefes de Estado y de Gobierno delMecanismo de Diálogo

y Concertación de Tuxtla, *Declaración Conjunta Sobre Crimen Organizado y Narcotráfico*, 5 December 2011, http://www.presidencia.gob.mx/2011/12/declaracion-conjunta-sobre-crimen-organizado-y-narcotrafico/.

20 Discussion between author and senior US official involved in drugs policy, February 2012.

21 Amie Ferrris-Rotman, 'Special Report: In Russia, a Glut of Heroin and Denial', Reuters, 25 January 2011.

22 *INCB Report 2004* (INCB: Vienna, 2004), pp. 23–5.

23 This suggestion was made in 2008 by the Senlis Council, now known as the International Council on Security and Development (ICOS).

24 Paul Collier, 'Breaking the Conflict Trap: Civil War and Development Policy', *World Bank Policy Research Reports* (New York: OUP USA, 2003), p. 3.

Conclusion

1 Han-zhu Qian, Joseph E. Schumacher, Huey T. Chen and Yu-HuaRuan, 'Injection Drug Use and HIV/AIDS in China: Review of Current Situation, Prevention and Policy Implications', *Harm Reduction Journal*, vol. 3, no. 4, 2006, http://www.harmreductionjournal.com/content/3/1/4.

2 Jamie Doward, 'Colombian President Calls for Global Rethink on Drugs', *Guardian*, 12 November 2012, http://www.guardian.co.uk/world/2011/nov/13/colombia-juan-santos-call-to-legalise-drugs; Robin Yapp, 'Mexican President Hints US Should Legalise Drugs', *Telegraph*, 20 September 2011, http://www.telegraph.co.uk/news/worldnews/centralamericaandthecaribbean/mexico/8777235/Mexican-president-hints-US-should-legalise-drugs.html.

3 'Guatemalan President Weighs Drug Legalization, Blames US for Not Reducing Consumption', *Washington Post*, 13 February 2012, http://www.washingtonpost.com/world/americas/us-embassy-in-guatemala-criticizes-presidents-proposal-to-legalize-drugs/2012/02/12/gIQAToif9Q_story.html.

4 Reuters, 'Dozens Killed in Mexico Prison Violence', 20 February 2012, http://www.france24.com/en/20120220-mexico-deadly-fight-breaks-out-rival-gangs-drug-cartels-monterray-prison.

Appendix

1   One example of a drug that is not subject to the regime as specified by the conventions is ketamine, which is used as a horse tranquilizer and as an alternative to compressed oxygen in anaesthetisation. It is now also abused by drug addicts, with serious consequences. The UNODC has passed resolutions that have been adopted by many countries and ketamine has been placed on national prohibition lists but remains unaccounted for in the conventions. The 1971 Convention was designed to accommodate new trends in drug use, particularly with regard to synthetic substances. If the mechanism provided for in the 1961 convention regarding the inclusion of new drugs into the schedules were more streamlined, then it would be easier to have an international drug policy that comprehensively dealt with drug abuse. Many observers point to the tension between those countries with large pharmaceutical sectors, generally developed Western nations, and those countries that were affected by the 1961 controls on natural substances, usually less-developed nations, as being the cause for the incompatibility of this treaty with the Single Act. These contradictions caused the European Parliament to commission a report in 2003 which essentially called for an overhaul of the three conventions currently in effect.

Adelphi books are published eight times a year by Routledge Journals, an imprint of Taylor & Francis, 4 Park Square, Milton Park, Abingdon, Oxfordshire OX14 4RN, UK.

A subscription to the institution print edition, ISSN 1944-5571, includes free access for any number of concurrent users across a local area network to the online edition, ISSN 1944-558X. Taylor & Francis has a flexible approach to subscriptions enabling us to match individual libraries' requirements. This journal is available via a traditional institutional subscription (either print with free online access, or online-only at a discount) or as part of the Strategic, Defence and Security Studies subject package or Strategic, Defence and Security Studies full text package. For more information on our sales packages please visit www.tandfonline.com/librarians_pricinginfo_journals.

2012 Annual Adelphi Subscription Rates			
Institution	£525	$924 USD	€777
Individual	£239	$407 USD	€324
Online only	£473	$832 USD	€699

Dollar rates apply to subscribers outside Europe. Euro rates apply to all subscribers in Europe except the UK and the Republic of Ireland where the pound sterling price applies. All subscriptions are payable in advance and all rates include postage. Journals are sent by air to the USA, Canada, Mexico, India, Japan and Australasia. Subscriptions are entered on an annual basis, i.e. January to December. Payment may be made by sterling cheque, dollar cheque, international money order, National Giro, or credit card (Amex, Visa, Mastercard).

For a complete and up-to-date guide to Taylor & Francis journals and books publishing programmes, and details of advertising in our journals, visit our website: http://www.tandfonline.com.

Ordering information:
USA/Canada: Taylor & Francis Inc., Journals Department, 325 Chestnut Street, 8th Floor, Philadelphia, PA 19106, USA. UK/Europe/Rest of World: Routledge Journals, T&F Customer Services, T&F Informa UK Ltd., Sheepen Place, Colchester, Essex, CO3 3LP, UK.

Advertising enquiries to:
USA/Canada: The Advertising Manager, Taylor & Francis Inc., 325 Chestnut Street, 8th Floor, Philadelphia, PA 19106, USA. Tel: +1 (800) 354 1420. Fax: +1 (215) 625 2940. UK/Europe/Rest of World: The Advertising Manager, Routledge Journals, Taylor & Francis, 4 Park Square, Milton Park, Abingdon, Oxfordshire OX14 4RN, UK. Tel: +44 (0) 20 7017 6000. Fax: +44 (0) 20 7017 6336.

The print edition of this journal is printed on ANSI conforming acid-free paper by Bell & Bain, Glasgow, UK.